The Joy of Text

'the fastest book ever written'

CORGI BOOKS

THE JOY OF TEXT
A CORGI BOOK : 0 552 14936 5

First publication in Great Britain

PRINTING HISTORY
Corgi edition published 2001

1 3 5 7 9 10 8 6 4 2

Corgi Books are published by Transworld Publishers,
61-63 Uxbridge Road, London W5 5SA,
a division of The Random House Group Ltd,
in Australia by Random House Australia (Pty) Ltd,
20 Alfred Street, Milsons Point, Sydney, NSW 2061, Australia,
in New Zealand by Random House New Zealand Ltd,
18 Poland Road, Glenfield, Auckland 10, New Zealand
and in South Africa by Random House (Pty) Ltd,
Endulini, 5a Jubilee Road, Parktown 2193, South Africa.

Printed and bound in Great Britain by
Clays Ltd, St Ives plc.

Foreword

Once upon a time, your mobile phone was only really mobile if you had a wheelbarrow to carry it around in. Today phones are getting smaller and lighter by the minute and people are doing a lot more with them than just talking. The dialling has stopped and the typing has started as text messaging has taken over the keyboards, becoming the coolest and trendiest new way of communicating with your mobile. R U Wiv it?

Text messaging or SMS is quick, cheap and can be a lot of fun, as you are about to discover in this unique book.

Introduced in 1995 as a way of allowing phone networks to communicate important service messages to their subscribers, over the past two years text messaging has caught the imagination of mobile phone users all over the world and is now used by over 70 per cent of them.

Over one billion text messages are now sent every month here in the UK. It is estimated that one hundred million of these are work related, which is rather disappointing until you realise that this means the other nine hundred million are nothing to do with work at all. U Sxy Thngs!

The secrecy element of sending a text message means that it is now the most popular way for teenagers to flirt and socialise with each other. In

December 2000, 756 million text messages were sent all over the world as people dumped the traditional Christmas card in favour of a seasonal text message. Mry Xms!

The peak hours for text messaging are strangely close to last orders, being between 10.30 and 11 at night, as people arrange their next social venue of the evening. This may also account for the wild abbreviations and crazy, easy to understand new spellings which have taken over the text language. C Wot I Mn? Slurring your words is a definite benefit when writing quick text messages!

On 9th June 2001, the BBC broadcast a highly successful themed night of programming based around text messaging. During the show they asked viewers, if they could send one text message to anyone, anywhere, who would it be to and what would they say – thus providing an instant snapshot of the hopes and wishes of the nation at that particular moment. Funny, poignant or just plain daft, some of those messages, along with the best, and cleanest, text jokes sent in to the BBC during the Joy Of Text are published here. Wr U Prt Of It? The messages have been printed exactly as they were texted in, so be prepared for some fairly unorthodox spelling.

Whether you are a text message maestro or an absolute beginner, you'll never look at your mobile phone in the same way again and this book is guaranteed to put a big ☺ on your face and your phone screen!

Lisa Clark

.ıll

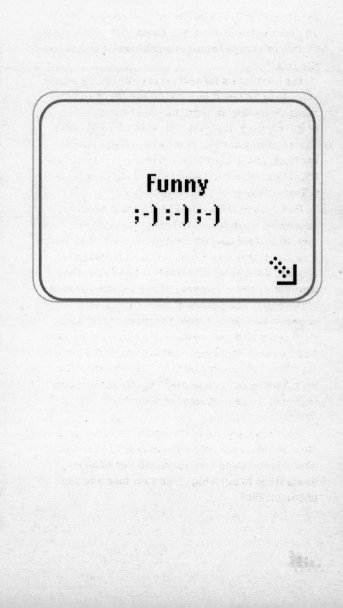

Funny
;-) :-) ;-)

```
     /)/)
    =(';')=
  ,,,(")(")"),,,
```

```
     //////
    ( o  o )
  oo0-(_)-0oo
  WOT? NO CREDIT
```

```
   /)/)      /)/)
  =(';')=   =(';')=
,,(")(")("),  ,(")(")(")","
   YOU   &   ME
```

```
   ww   ///
  ( '"  "' )
  (//)  (//)
 ⁻oo⁻⁻⁻oo⁻
```

```
  ⟨( , , )⟩
  ( (..) )
  YOU SWINE!
```

9

Uve got Sex
Appeal...Uve got
Style...Uve got
Intelligence...&
Uve got Class...
Uve got D face..&
uve got D body..&

ive got the wrong
number. SORRY

```
. +.*.+.*.+.
*.+.*.+.*.+*
Abracadabra
. +.*.+.*.+.
*.+.*.+.*.+*
```

nope, ur
still ugly!

1
message
received

1
sexy friend
sent it

1
monkey is
reading it

1
monkey is
angry

1
sexy friend
is smiling

1
monkey is still
reading it

Ha!Ha!Ha!

This msg can only
be read by a SEXY
person:

🖱

Try again...

🖱

Nothing? Sorry, i
guess your just
not SEXY...

🖱

HEY! Don't force it
ugly, get lost!

, ;'(.) (.)' ;
;' ;. (o o) . ;' ;
(; ;(___)' ; ;)
«; : ;⎯; : ; »

🖱

wot a great mobile
u have, its got a
mirror !

Press down if u
dont like me

I cant believe u did that !

& again ? I can't
believe you !

how rude

Why are you still
doing it ?

Oh Im really
hurt now !

Swine!

```
/),,/)
(' ; ')
(,,)-(,,)
```
HOPPY EASTER !

After John Prescott's egg throwing
incident, the press thinks he should get
a bodyguard. It was only a little egg,
what do they think he needs, soldiers?

Two cows in a field
One cow says "Have you heard
about this mad cow disease?"
The other thinks and replies "Yep but
it doesn't affect us rabbits"

Who Wants 2 B A
£MILLIONAIRE£
Let's play?

Q.Nobody likes u
cos u r a: A.Idiot B.Fool
C.Stupid D.Slow

50/50 Phone a friend?

RING ME! I'LL TELL U!

GOD created the
world in SIX days
But it took him
CENTURIES…

To Create
SOMEONE…

As "HOT"

As "SEXY"

As "LOVEABLE"

* .. as ME ..*

What city has the largest
rodent population?
Hamsterdam
From Jason D

The japanese have banned all animal
movements after discovering
droppings in the bedding in Tokyo.
They beleive it could be a
case of Futon Mouse.

how do u occupy an idiot?

press down

press up!

Save the rain forests
Squash a woodworm

You can always tell when a manis going
to say somthing intelligent. He starts his
sentence with, "a woman once
told me!!!!!"

What do you call an unemployed jester?
Nobodys fool

The Joy of Text

Teenage boys aren't the only ones to use their phones to get dates. A pan-European survey reveals that a massive eighty per cent of German men have used SMS to chat somebody up, while an astonishing six per cent of Europeans claim to have been taking phone sex to extremes by texting during 'sexual acts' with someone else. (How? And why?) A fifth of Finnish women do it in the sauna — send saucy text messages, that is — and fifteen per cent of British women have ended a relationship with a text message ('yr dmpd' is brief but undeniably to the point). No wonder so many relationships are on the rocks when ninety per cent of British men admit to lying about where they are in messages. Irish men don't come out well, either: twenty per cent of Irish women have had SMS marriage proposals, but sixty per cent of Irish men use messaging to swap stories about their sex lives. What the survey doesn't reveal is how many of those stories were made up.

Loading the Babe meter.....

5%

17%

26%

57%

78%

99%

100%

COMPLETE

Processing data..

ANALYSIS COMPLETE

U R A 100% Gorgeous Babe xxx

What flies and wobbles?
A jellycopter

I N V U 4 U R A Q T
I envy you for you are a cutie

Did u hear bout the nu mag for
married men by Playboy?
It has the same pictures month after
month after month after month
after month

2 MEN R FISHING. A FUNERAL MARCH
GOES BY. THE 1ST MAN PLACES HIS HAT ON
HIS CHEST. 2ND MAN-'THATS NICE' 1ST
MAN-ITS THE LEAST I CAN DO WE WERE
MARRIED 25 YEARS

Why did the farmer win a nobel prize?
Because he was out standing
in his field!!!

What do u call James Bond in the bath?
Bubble 07. Love Harry Aged 10
Romford.

:(:) Why did the jelly baby go to
school? Because it wanted to be
a smarty.   ha ha from helen d

Don't anthropomorphize computers -
they hate it.

do u take me 2 b ur lawful textm8,2
have and 2 hold 4 dirty jokes and saucy
jokes, in text messaging and in
poorsignal till low battery do us part?

Send To: Bill Gates Message: Reply To
Sender With Bank Account PIN No.

What is a zebra?
26 sizes larger than A bra.

What did Mrs Christmas say to Mr
Christmas during the thunder storm?
Look @ the rain deer!

An Englishman, even if he is alone,
forms an orderly queue of one.

What do u call a dog with no legs?
It doesn't matter wot u call him
he ain't gonna cum.
Oliver Howes

For Sale - complete set of Encyclopedia
Britanica. 74 Volumes, good
condition, £1000 ONO. No longer needed,
got married, the wife knows
bloody everything.

I went to buy some camouflage trousers
the other day but i could'nt find any.

If ignorance is bliss, WHY are there so
many unhappy people?

If love is blind, then why is
lingerie so popular?!

Why did the cannibal rush over to
the cafeteria? He heard children
were half price.
From Jason D

Mary Had A little lamb she tied it to a pylon, 10,000 volts up its bum turned its wool to nylon.

WHAT DO YOU CALL A DINOSAUR WITH
LARGE HAEMORRHOIDS?
A MEGASORARSE.

FOR SALE:
1 gran reconditioned heart, body needs
great attention nearest offer or will
swap for pokemon cards.
(Leanne, Manchester, 17)

Why don't lobsters share?
Because they're shellfish

WHY DO TELETUBBIES GO 2 THE
LOO 2GETHER?
BECAUSE THEY ONLY HAVE 1 TINKY WINKY

If a big fat man comes late night in your room and wants to pack you in his bag, do not worry. I told Santa, that I want you for Christmas!

I'm an alien I've transformed into your phone and as your reading this I'm having sex with your finger. I know you like it because you're smiling

When the going gets tough, the tough take Prozac.

Mary had a little lamb and the doctor fainted.

I'm pink therefore i'm spam

How do you keep an idiot in suspense? I'll tell you tomorrow!

I wish i was a glow worm,
A glow worm's never glum
How can you be unhappy
When the sun shines out yorbum?

If barbie is so popular why do u
have to buy her friends?

. An ant!

A-Ur Attractive
B-Ur Buff
C-Ur Charming
D-Ur Delicious
E-Ur Exciting
F-Ur Funny
G-Ur Gorgeous
H-Ur Heavenly
I-I'm
J-Just
K-Kidding
L-Loser

Roses are red violit are blue a face like
yours belongs to the zoo

Love is in the Airwaves

Welcome to romance in the third millennium. The traditional love tokens of red roses, expensive Belgian chocolates and handmade cards are out: this year SMS has become the favoured way of getting sloppy with your loved one. On Valentine's Day 2001, the British sent around fifty million text messages, smashing the previous record of ten million text messages sent on New Year's Eve. The most common messages sent included the stunningly original 'i luv u', 'b my vlntn' and 'hppy vlntns dy' (for some reason 'im yr snggly bnnykns' doesn't feature in the top ten). Around only twelve million Valentine's cards were delivered by the Post Office – that's under a quarter of the number of text messages that were sent on February 14th. So is the Valentine's text message now officially more romantic than the traditional posted Valentine, or are we just a nation who couldn't be bothered to buy cards?

What is the second longest word ever?!
SMILES
coz it has got mile between the
1st and the last letter

A member of the bomb squad has a
saying on the back of his t-shirt. I'm a
Bomb Technichian, if u see me running,
try 2 keep up.

Two cows in a field. One says to the
other."What about this mad cow
disease, then?"
The other one says "Doesn't affect me
mate i'm a duck".

If religion is the opium of the people, is
going to Ibiza a pilgrimage?

A bear walks into a bar and says
"Can I have a pint of lager
and.....................
a packet of crisps please."
The barman says "Why the paws?"

The jogger who overslept found himself
running late.

A girl phoned me the other day and
said…"Come on over, there's nobody
home." I went over. Nobody was home.

Woman asks a barman "can i have a
double entendre please", so the
barman gives her one…

When The Red Boat and the Blue Boat
sank, the survivers were Marooned
(ShyFox)

Why didn't the skeleton go 2 the disco?
Because he had no body 2 go wit

If at first you don't succeed, skydiving
is not for you.

Two aerials meet on a roof - fell in love
and got married. The ceremony was
terrible, but the reception was brilliant!

Two cannibals were eating a clown.
One says to the other "Does this taste
funny to you?"

I had a ploughman's lunch
the other day.
He wasn't very happy.

WOT WAKES SHEEP UP IN THE MORNING?
A lamb clock

WOT DO U CALL A GROUP OF 10 BARBIES
WAITING AT BUS STOP??
BARBIE-QUEUE!

WHAT DO U CALL A WOMAN WHO PLAYS POOL
WHILST BALANCING A PINT ON HER HEAD?
BEATRIX POTTER

WHY DO GORILLAS HAVE BIG NOSTRILS?
COS THEY'VE GOT BIG FINGERS.

Y DID THE MAN CITY MANAGER HAND OUT
LIGHTERS 2 HIS TEAM?
CAUSE THEY KEPT LOSING ALL
THEIR MATCHES!
SEAN DEVERSON IPSWICH

WHO VARNISHED THE DECKS OF THE TITANIC?
LEONARDO DE'CUPRINOL!
xRIGGZ :D

HOW DO U GET PIKACHU ON A BUS?
"POKE EM ON".
FAE DAVIE IN ABERDEEN.

Theres three mice in airing cupboard
which ones in the army?
That one sat on the tank

Why do cats not shave?
Cuz 80% prefer Whiskers!!

WHY DID BOBBY ROBSON HAVE THE PITCH AT
ST JAMES PARK FLOODED?
So he could bring on his sub!! HA HA!!
FROM EMILY GILL FROM DONCASTER!

I HEAR YORKSHIRE CLUBBERS HAVE TAKEN TO
USING DENTAL SYRINGES TO INJECT ECSTACY
DIRECTLY INTO THEIR MOUTH THIS
DANGEROUS PRACTICE IS KNOWN AS
E BY GUM

WHAT DO YOU CALL A VICAR ON
A MOTOR BIKE?
REV.

DID U HEAR ABOUT THE DUTCH MAN WITH THE
INFLATABLE SHOES?
HE POPPED HIS CLOGS!
FROM TOM IN CHESTERFIELD,

Chelsea signed 2 players from iceland.
Ranieri said if they r no good he will
try sainsburys.

HOW DO YOU COMONICATE WITH A FISH?
DROP IT A LINE

What do u get i f u cross a
policeman with an artist?
A brush with the law.
From the Lyndseys in Strood,Kent.

HOW DO U MAKE A DOG DRINK?
PUT IT IN A BLENDER

Y is tigger always dirty.......Because he
plays with poo

Y DID THE JELLY BEAN GO 2 SKOL?
BCOZ IT WANTED 2 B A SMARTIE!
FROM SOPH IN BELFAST :o)

WHERE DOES KYLIE MINOGUE GET
HER KEBABS?
JASON'S DONNER VAN

31

What do elephants have for dinner?
An hour just like the rest of the animals

HEARD OF THE VEGETARIAN CANNIBAL?
HE ONLY ATE SWEDES

WOT ANIMAL DO U LOOK LIKE WHEN U GET
OUT THE SHOWER .....A LITTLE BEAR

Shakespeare walks into a pub and
orders a pint. The barman says I can't
serve you you're Bard

WOT DO U CALL A DONKEY WITH NO BRAIN?
MY BROTHER
FROM SARAH

How does Bob Marley like
his sandwiches?
Wi Jammin'

A snail is just a yuppie slug

WHAT DO U CALL A TRIPLE BARREL
SHOTGUN........... A TRIFLE

WHAT DO YOU CALL A HANDCUFED MAN?
TRUSTWORTHY. :-)JEMMA MIDDLETON

WOTS A DINNER LADYS FAVOURITE PUDDING?
APPLE GRUMBLE!

WHAT DO CALL A FILM STAR THATS
LOST HIS DOG?
MICHAEL DOGLESS

HI ULRIKA ITS MATT ELWELL FROM THE
WEST MIDS HERE IS MY JOKE
WHAT DO YOU CALL A GIRL WHO GAMBLES?
BETTY.
BYE

Wot does a constipated
mathematiacian do?
Work it out with a pencil!

TWO CANNIBALS ARE AT A WEDDING ONE
TURNS TO THE AND SAYS I DONT LIKE THE
LOOK OF YOUR MOTHER IN LAW!..WELL LEAVE
HER ALONE AND JUST EAT THE CHIPS!!!!

WHAT DO MEXICANS HAVE UNDER
THEIR CARPETS?
UNDERLAY!UNDERLAY!
JAY MILLER

What do you call a snowman with a
suntan? .... a puddle
from gail

IN CASE OF FIRE READ THIS MESSAGE...
NOT NOW U FOOL ONLY IN CASE OF FIRE

Be My Valen-Thai-ne

The romantic population of Thailand managed to disrupt an entire mobile phone network on Valentine's Day by sending love messages to each other. Apparently, messaging started as normal in the morning, but by the afternoon the computer system controlling the network was clogged up with 200 per cent more text messages than it normally has to cope with. Voice calls became jammed, SMS went down and eventually the whole service toppled and crashed for two days. You could say that's real proof of the power of love. . .

WHAT DYA CALL A NUN WITH A WASHING
MACHINE ON ER HEAD? . . .
SISTER MATIC
DAN FROM STOKE

A man walks into a butchers,
excuse me he asks have you got
a sheeps head?
No, says the butcher it's how I
brush my hair.

What's the maximum penalty
for bigamy?
Two mothers-in-law.

WHAT DO YOU GET IF YOU CROSS A SKUNK
WITH A BOOMERANG?
A BAD SMELL YOU CANT GET RID OF
FROM DIANE - NEW PITSLIGO

A white horse went in2 a pub the
barman said iv got a whisky named
after u the horse said well give us a
double Dobbin then.

2 FAT BLOKES IN A PUB, 1 SAYS "YOUR ROUND" THE OTHER SAYS "SO ARE YOU, YOU FAT GIT!!!"

WHAT DO U CALL A FISH WITH NO EYES?
-A FSH!!
FROM THOMAS, AGE 7
FROM WARRINGTON.

WHATS THE FASTEST CAKE IN THE WORLD?
SCONE

What do you call a spider with no legs?
A currant.

WHY DO ELEPHANTS HAVE BIG EARS?
BECAUSE NODDY WONT PAY THE RANSOM

Whats pink and mows the lawn?..........................
A PRAWN MOWER!

Wot did the Spanish fireman
call his twin sons?
Hose A & Hose B!

I was arrested the other night & the
pman said have u got a police record? 2
which i replied ive got walking on the
moon will that do.

THE MAN THAT WROTE THE SONG THE HOKEY
COKEY DIED LAST WEEK BUT THEY HAD A REAL
PROBLEM GETTING HIM IN THE COFFIN : THEY
PUT HIS LEFT LEG IN HIS LEFT LEG OUT…!

What do you get when you drop a piano
down a mine shaft?
A flat minor.
riccardo & natalie-sheffield.

Police found a man dead in a ice cream
van today covered in chocolate sauce
and hundreds and thousands. police say
he topped himself! ; ->>

Why can't the leopard leave the zoo?
Because he always gets spotted!
From Amy Franks in Deal.

What part of France has got more
than one toilet?
Toulouse.

2 COWS IN A FIELD 1 SAYS "MOO" THE OTHER
SAID "I WAS JUST ABOUT 2 SAY THAT"

WHY DID THE SKELETON CROSS THE ROAD?
TO GET TO THE BODY SHOP. FROM PHILIP
BLAYNEY

WOT DID THE BABY CORN SAY 2 THE
MUMMY CORN?
WERS POPCORN.

A sheriff puts up a wanted poster which
has a man wearing a paperbag on his
head. And a man asks what is he
wanted for? Ans. for rustling…

**WHAT DO U GET WHEN U CROSS A SNOWMAN
AND A VAMPIRE? FROSTBITE**

**WHAT DO U CALL A SKELETON WHO
SLEEPS A LOT?
LAZY BONES.**

**DID YOU HEAR ABOUT THE MAN WHO
NICKED THE CALENDAR?
HE GOT 12 MONTHS**

**How many text maniacs does it take 2
change a light bulb?
50, 1 to change it + 49 to work out the txt
shorthand that tells u how 2.
Jase, Thame, Oxfordshire.**

**Have you seen the new christmas toy.
Divorced barbie. Comes with all
kens accessories**

SMS Service

The concept of spreading the word has gone one step further, as the Gospel Youth Church of Hanover has put together Germany's first SMS church service called 'God and the World in 160 Characters' for young mobile phone users. Each service is split into five 160-character parts: a greeting, a reading from the Bible, a sermon, prayers and a final blessing, with pauses between each section to give the recipient time to reflect on the message. Church leaders are hoping that subscribers will also text back their own prayers to be read out in church. God moves in mysterious ways.

TWO OLD LADIES SAT ON A PARK BENCH A
STREAKER RAN PAST ONE OLD LADY HAD A
STROKE THE OTHER COULDENT REACH.

WHAT DO U CALL A SKODA WITH A SUNROOF?
A SKIP

How do u keep a txtr in suspence?
I'll tell u l8r

THERES 2 COWS IN A FIELD WHICH ONE HAS
FOOT AND MOUTH?
THE ONE THATS ON FIRE

WHAT HAPPENED WHEN THE FROGS CAR
BROKE DOWN?
IT GOT TOAD AWAY

WHY ARE ALL DUMB BLONDE JOKES
ONE-LINERS?
....
SO MEN CAN UNDERSTAND THEM.

WOT DO U DO IF A BLONDE THROWS A
GRENADE AT U?
TAKE THE PIN OUT AND THROW IT BACK!

A man is like a lava lamp; good to look
at but not very bright!! Nicola
Neighbour from Harlow in Essex

WHICH KING OF ENGLAND
INVENTED THE FIRE PLACE ?
ALFRED THE GRATE

Have u heard about the magic tractor?
that went down a country road and
turned into a field

WHAT LIES AT THE BOTTOM OF THE SEA AND
SHIVERS? A NERVOUS WRECK! FROM JENNY

Did you hear about the Dyslexic
Kamikazi pilot who bombed
Poole harbour

What was the orange doing on the
table? Not much just looking round.

Baby i'm just like an American Express
card - u shudn't go home without me!

Why should you never undress
in front of a Pokemon?
Incase they Pikachu.

HAUE U HEARD ABOUT THE CRAB WHO
WENT INTO A NIGHT CLUB?
HE PULLED A MUSSEL

WHY DONT LIVERPOOL HAVE A
DRINK AT HALFTIME?
COS ALL THE MUGS ARE IN THE STANDS
& AND THE CUPS ARE AT OLD TRAFFORD.

I want to die peacefully in my sleep like
my grandfather... Not screaming in
terror like his passengers!

Two cows in a field what 1s on holiday?
The 1 with the wee calf....Sent by pam
irvine scotland ;-)

Wot do u get if u pour boiling water
down a rabbit hole? Hot cross bunnies.

WHAT DO MONSTERS EAT AT SEA?
FISH AND SHIPS!
MATT FROM BATH

Dracula woz out walking 1 night
when chicken legs sausages and
sandwiches fell on him. With his dying
breath he sighed oh no its buffet
the vampire slayer

Wasssup?......
The opposite of down!

A MAN WALKS INTO A DOCTORS WITH A PIECE
OF LETTUCE HANGING OUT OF HIS BUM "THAT
LOOKS NASTY" SAYS DOC. "THATS JUST THE
TIP OF THE ICEBERG"   SAYS MAN.

WHY WAS THE FOOTBALL PITCH WET?
BCOZ THE FOOT BALLERS KEPT DRIBBLING!

WHAT SORT OF SHOES DO FROGS
WHERE ON THE BEACH?
OPEN TOAD SANDALS.
BY LOUISE ROBERTS.

Why is cinderela a poor
basketball player?....
BECAUSE SHE HAD A PUMPKIN FOR A COACH!

WHY CAN'T A CAR PLAY FOOTBALL?
COS ITS ONLY GOT ONE BOOT ON
FROM CARRIE IN KIRKBY NEAR MANSFIELD
NOTTINGHAM

THIS IS LAURA ROSE ALLWOOD SENDING TWO
JOKES. WHY HAS BUGS BUNNY GOT LARGE
EARS? BECAUSE HE'S A RABBIT. HOW DO YOU
GET MILK FROM A CAT? TAKE IT'S
SAUCER AWAY.

whats green and sits in the corner? the
incredible sulk.

HOW MANY PSYCHOLOGISTS DOES IT TAKE TO
CHANGE A LIGHTBULB? ONE, THE LIGHTBULB
HAS TO WANT TO CHANGE!

A PANDA GOES INTO A RESTERAUNT. HE EATS
HIS MEAL THEN SHOOTS THE WAITER. THE
MANAGER SAYS U CAN'T DO THAT, THE PANDA
SAID YES I CAN LOOK IN THE DICTIONARY....
SO THE MANAGER LOOKS IN THE DICTIONARY
AND THE DEFINITION OF PANDA SAYS... EATS
SHOOTS AND LEAVES!!! :-)

A SHOP HAD A PAIR OF RIDING BOOTS FOR
SALE A MAN SAID TO THE ASSISTANT THOSE
ARENT RIDING BOOTS THE ASSITANT SAID
WELL YOU TRY WALKING IN THEM THEN.

Sex is like Nokia (connecting people),
Like Nike (just do it),
Like Pepsi(ask for more),
Like Samsung (everyone is invited)
And Like me (too good to be true)!

What's the difference between a blonde
and a supermarket trolly?
The supermarket trolly has a mind
of it's own!!

Texan: You know you can board a train
ride for 24 hours and still be in Texas.
Brit: Yup we have that problem
all the time.

Guru: "A million years is like a minute; a
million dollars like a cent"
Disciple: "Master can you give
me a cent?"
Guru: "In a minute"

WHY DID THE BLONDE GET FIRED
FROM THE M&M FACTORY?
FOR THROWING OUT ALL THE W'S!

WHAT STAYS HOT IN THE FRIDGE?
MUSTARD

what is small, furry and wicked at
sword digits? a mouse-keteer

Dis is da 121 customer service, we must
inform you dat your breath is interfering
wid our reception so cud you please
purchase a 'Wrigley's Extra' for yourself.

A GHOST WENT IN2 A PUB AT MIDNIGHT +
ASKED THE BARMAN 4 A WHISKY. "SORRY
SIR," REPLIED THE BARMAN "WE ARENT
ALLOWED 2 SERVE SPIRITS AFTER CLOSIN
TIME" KAYLEIGH

WHY DO ONLY 10% OF MEN MAKE IT 2
HEAVEN? IF THEY ALL WENT, IT
WOULD B HELL!

Press down if u think lim buff..
I KNEW IT!
lim 2 good
Wot can I say!
Still pressin?
U must really love me!
O stop it!
Well, wot can i say??

whats did one worm say to another
when he was late home? why in earth
are you late?

WHY IS THE SAND WET?
BECAUSE THE SEA WEED

I GOT A NEW SHAMPOO TODAY, IT WAS
CALLED WASH AND GO SO I WASHED MY HAIR
AND IT WENT. FROM JENNY NEWMAN FROM
WEST CROYDON

HOW DOES THE MAN IN THE MOON CUT HIS
HAIR?   ECLIPSE IT!!

On a cold night u only have 1 match.
There is a gas oven, a coal burning fire
& an oil lamp. Which must u light 1st?
The match. Duh! Lydia Parsonson.

WHAT SHAPE DO PEARS GO WHEN
EVERYTHING GOES WRONG?
A PUZZLING QUESTION! :)

2 PEANUTS WERE WALKIN DOWN THE RD.
1 WAS A-SALTED!!!!

A LORRYLOAD OF WIGS AVE BEEN STOLEN ON
THE M1, THE POLICE R COMBING THE AREA

A man walked in to a fish un chip shop
and said cod and chips twice . The
woman said alright i heard u the first
time !!!!! laura wilkes age 11 thank u

There was two bags of crisps walking on the pavement then a car pulled up and said 'do you want a lift?' The crisps said 'no we are Walkers'

2 men r in a bar celebrating. The barman asks "Wot's the occasion?" The men replie "We finished a puzzle in 2 months and it said 2-4 years on the box!"
Chris Palmer

Why was the computer in pain?
Because it had slipped a disk.
By Vanessa Curry From Newcastle

WHAT VEG CAN PLAY SNOOKER?
CUE-CUMBER!
FROM LISA PURVIS OF MIDDLESBROUGH

A MAN WITH 2 LEFT FEET WALKS INTO A SHOE SHOP, AND ASKED FOR WHAT?
A PAIR OF FLIP FLIPS.
SARAH. AGED 12

WHAT DO U CALL A WOMAN BETWEEN
2 POSTS? ANNETTE

WHY ARE COOKS CRUEL?
THEY BEAT EGGS, WHIP CREAM
AND BATTER FISH.

WHAT IS THE LONGEST WORD IN
THE DICTONARY?
ELASTIC CAUSE ITS STRECHY

FROM MY G/SON AGED 3 WHAT DO U CALL A
SHEEP WITHOUT LEGS?
A CLOUD

What do u do if a blonde
thros a pin at u?
run, she has a grenade in her mouth

DID U HEAR ABOUT THE WOMAN WHO
SWALLOWED A BTLE. OF HARPIC? ****
IT SENT HER CLEAN ROUND THE BEND. Hf Hf.
FROM H. HOLMAN. CONSETT CO DURHAM. :-)

B. I. T. C. H.

Beautiful

Intelligent

Talented

Cute

Honest

r u smiling now?

**WHATS THE BEST TIME TO GO
TO THE DENTIST?
TOOTH HURTY**

WHAT DO U CALL A BLIND DINOSAUR?
DO U THINKHESAURUS ...
BY KAREN ACKERLEY FROM TIMPERLEY XXX

WHY DO GIRAFFES HAVE LONG NECKS?
BECAUSE THEY HAVE SMELLY FEET.
FROM DOMINIQUE WHO IS 2

WHY WAS THE LITTLE EGYPTIAN BOY
CONFUSED ? BECAUSE HIS DADDY
WAS A MUMMY.

SPELL HUNGRY HORSE IN 4
LETTERS*****M*T*G*G

What happened to the bloke who
injected curry in to himself?...He went
in to a Korma!
Laura B. Cheltenham

There is a fire at the exchange. Please
put your phone in a bucket of water to
help with the fire fighting effort.

Why did the cat eat cheese?
So it could sit by a mousehole with
baited breath!

Men are like.....computers
Hard to figure out and never have
enough memory.

Why do little boys whine?
Because they're practicing to be men.

Wot did the grape say when sum1
stood on it?
Nothin it just gave out a little whine!

How many letters are in the Alphabet??
Nineteen. Because ET went Home on a
UFO and the FBI went after him!

How many men does it take to
change a lightbulb??
Just one, he holds the bulb and waits
for the world to revolve around him!

Why are Blonde jokes one-liners?
So brunettes can understand them.

Where does Saddam Hussein
keep his CDs?
In a-rack (Iraq)!
Yes I know its pathetic but its the only
one liner joke I can remember!

what do you call a
greenfly with no legs ?
a bogey

Doctor, Doctor My little boy has just
swallowed a roll of film!
Hmmmm. Let's hope nothing develops.
Sean Purcell

WHY DUS BATMAN SRCH 4 WORMS
2 FEED HIS ROBIN.

ANYONE KNOW WHO ACTUALLY
LET THE DOGS OUT? LIAM ;)

I used to like tractors, but now I'm an
(ex)tractor fan

wh@ noise d porkupines make when
they kiss?
ouch!

Though i seldom msg u. I always carry
ur photo with me!!
* * * * * * * *
* ")".."(" *
*   ((..))   *
* * * * * * * *

see how sweet hehehe!

knock knock
who's there?
Alex
alex who?
Alexplain later,just let me in

What day does a fish hate? Fry day.
From Jason D

Ramadan

The most holy month in the Islamic calendar, Ramadan is the time when Muslims fast from sunrise to sunset and particular prayer times must be observed. But as it is based on the lunar calendar, it can be difficult for British Muslims to know the exact dates of the beginning and end of the holy month and what times of day the calls to prayer should take place. In Islamic countries the muezzin sounds the summons to prayer, but this isn't allowed in most areas of Britain. So an ingenious solution has been found: the SMS summons. Not only does the service tell subscribers the exact dates of Ramadan, it can alert you every time you should be at prayer. It will also tell you when sunrise and sunset officially occur in the nearest major city to your own location so that you can fast at the right times. And when GPS becomes a standard feature of mobile phones, it will even be able to point you in the right direction to Mecca so you know which way to pray.

Y is abbreviation such a long word?

One Tequila
two tuqiela
three quteila
floor!

What do you call a cat that lives in the
desert? Sandy Claws.
From Jason D

I've told you ten million times
to stop exaggerating!
from russell carswell, l'pool

Y WOMEN R LIKE COMPUTERS 1)no one
really understands dem 2)all ur
mistakes r stored in their memory
3)u find urself spendin all ur money
on accessories for dem!

Y MEN R LIKE COMPUTERS 1)dey r useless
until u turn dem on 2)dey have lots of
data but r still clueless 3)as soon as u
pick 1, a better model cums on
the market!

WOT DO U CAL TH FASTEST FISH
IN TH WORLD?
A MOTOR PIKE!!!

I'm thinking of going into farming but I
don`t know what field to go into

She's so blonde she spent an hour
looking at a can of orange juice
because it said "concentrate".
by Ben Munns

My wife dresses 2 kill- the only
problem is that she cooks in
the same manner

What did one magnet say to the other
magnet? I find you very attractive.
From Jason D

@(-_-)@   princess leia's gonna get ya.
lol

why was 6 afraid of 7 ?
Coz' 7 8 9

WHERE DO VAMPIERS KEEP THEIR MONEY?
IN A BLOOD BANK.?

How do u make holy water?
Boil the Hell out of it!!

What did the elephant say to
the naked man?
How can u breathe through that!

What do you call a donkey
with three legs?
Wonkey!

Suezanne, What do you call a
female magician ?
Trixie! From 7 year old stephanie.

Mick the taking is someone that realise
you point this at is it
(now read it backwards)

A woman asked a man why he was so
shallow the man answered back and
said that he didnt think of himself as
shallow more as selectively deep

Hey, which animals were thr
last 2 leave the ark?
The elephants- they were
packing their trunks!
Bye..

63

What do you do when ur trying to kep
the sms shrt nd uv got to meet n
Llanfairpwllgwyngyllgogerychwyrndrob
wyll-llantysiliogogogoch? - Emma
(Wales)xx

What happens if u get scared half 2
death... twice?
- Scott, Sheffield

How do ya keep an idiot amused?
Tell em teh watch this message
until it goes away!

A boy had a test his mum asked him
'were the questions alright the boy said
yeah it was the answers i had trouble
with!' Shanando ;-P no.1

WHY DID THE LOBSTER BLUSH? CAUSE THE
SEA WEED :B) FROM SCREECH HACKETT IN
CORNWALL AGE 17

Video games dont affect kids - If
Pacman had affected us as kids we'd all
be running around in darkened rooms,
munching pills and listening to
repetitive music!

* * * * * * *
Phone error:
User is a knob.
* * * * * * *

Bald man: "Draw sum rabbits on my
head" Hairdresser: "Y?"   Bald man:
"From a distance they'll look
like hares ! ! !"

WOT HAVE MAN UTD & A 3 POINT PLUG GOT IN
COMMON? THEY'RE BOTH USELESS IN EUROPE

###8-(BAD HAIR DAY!!!

what's green and goes round and round
at 60 miles an hour ?   a mouldy frog
in a liquidiser. from samantha stubbs

What do u call a man who prefers his
phone to his girlfriend ? A txt maniac ;o)

There were two cows in a field, daisy
and mabel, and daisy said to mabel,
'i have been artifically made pregnant'
'no thats amazing', 'no straight up no
bull !!!!!!!!'

What did the fish say when he hit a
concrete wall..? Dam.

U're such a goodfriend!! If we were the
only 2 survifors on a sinking ship and
there was only 1 life jacket
left......................id really miss u

I dont suffer from insanity I enjoy every
minute of it .

3 Monkey's escape from a zoo. The first
was seen eating burger, The 2nd was
seen drinking pepsi and the 3rd was
seen reading this MESSAGE.

Your village called, their idiot
is missing.

A BRAIN & BATTERY WALK IN A PUB, THE
BARMAN SAYS I'M NOT SERVING U 2 COS UR
OUT OF UR HEAD & HE'S ABOUT TO START
SOMETHING!!!

Y DO 90% OF MARRAIGE'S FAIL? BECAUSE THE
BRIDE DOSE'NT MARRY THE BEST MAN

HOW CAN YOU TELL IF A BLOND HAS USED
YOUR COMPUTER--- TIPPEX ON THE SCREEN.

What do you call a man who
does everything at top speed
Max

Bring It Down

The Filipinos have always been fairly vocal and passionate about politics, but the National Telecommunications Commission in the Philippines was inundated with complaints in 2001 about subversive text messages in the run-up to the country's general election. The government decided it would have to get involved and demanded a crack-down on malicious or obscene texters, insisting that their phones should be disconnected from the network after candidates running for the Senate complained about being the subject of libellous text messages. This may seem like an over-reaction, but Philippine politicians have good reason to be wary of SMS. Although their laws ban the transmission of anything which could be construed as rumour-mongering, obscene, or anything which may disrupt public order, the country's former President, Joseph Estrada, is believed to have been overthrown by the power of SMS: the simple text message helped muster the mass anti-Presidential demonstration of a million Filipinos which forced Estrada to flee the Presidential Palace. But it wasn't all bad news for Senate candidates: some politicians decided to take the bull by the horns and used SMS to text 'vote 4 me' messages to mobile phone users. In fact, canvassers in Britain decided to follow their example and texted supporters with 'X 4 US'-style messages in the run-up to the 2001 UK general election.

But the Filipinos are renowned for being text-crazy, so

SMS can be a powerful tool. Land-line telephone service in the Philippines is very patchy and Internet connection is costly, but mobile phones are relatively inexpensive and texting is very cheap. (It was free, but the network had to introduce token charges after they were swamped with messages – 18 million a day, which worked out at an average of 26 per customer!) People text each other from restaurants, coffee bars, cars (even while driving, according to the police), religious services – one girl noticed mourners texting at her father's wake – and apparently texting even goes on in the battlefield. Troops fighting guerrillas in the island of Mindanao took their mobiles with them so they could keep in touch with their families, and some made their way into enemy hands. The rebels were quick to tap their way into the stored numbers, and started texting insults to the soldiers. 'It's childish,' said the general in charge of the troops, 'and it's the lighter side of this war, but who knows, perhaps it's better that they fight by texting.'

What do get if you come across
Eminem and Posh Spice
Answer-A Real Slim Lady

Man walks in2 a butcher, and asks 4 a
pound of sausages. The butcher says
"No-it's kilos now." Man says "Fine-i'll
have a pound of kilos, then."
HRH King Col.

if they can put 1 man on the moon, why
cant put them all up there,

WHAT TRANSPORT DO FISH USE? MOTOR-PIKE
& SIDE-CARP! FROM JO IN STOKE-ON-TRENT.

WHAT DO YOU CALL A PUB ON MARS? A
MARS BAR

WHAT DO YOU CALL A WOMEN WITH ONE
LEG:ANSWER EILEEN

WHAT DO U CALL A CAT WHO JUST
SWALLOWED A DUCK? --------- A DUCK
FILLED FATTY PUSS!

a boy walked into a bakers and asked
'can i have a wasp please?'
the baker said 'what? this is a bakers!?'
the boy said 'well, there is one in the
window'

How do u make an apple puff? Chase it
round the garden!

WADYA GET IF YOU DIAL
07870969718078709697180787069718
A BLISTER ON UR FNGER

Why did the tomato blush? because he
saw the salad dressing! ha ha ha...tb
chris from Colchester

WHY DID THE BAKER GET AN ELECTRIC
SHOCK?HE STOOD ON A BUN AND THE
CURRENT RAN UP HIS LEG!"
SAM WILSON, MORECAMBE.

What did the blonde say when a bloke
blew in her ear?thanx for the refill!
From mark

WHATS A HORSES FAVOURITE
PROGRAMME?NEIGH-BOURS BETHAN
ROBERTS ANGELSEA NORTH WALES

THERE WOZ A £10 NOTE ON THE FLOOR- WHO
PICKS IT UP, A PERFECT MAN, A PERFECT
WOMAN OR FATHER CHRISTMAS
+A PERFECT MAN BECAUSE THE OTHER
2 DONT EXIST

Who was the first person to
have a shell suit .
Answer humty dumty.

How does good king wenceslas like his pizza? Deep pan crisp and even

WHAT DO U GET WHEN U CROSS
AN ELEPHANT AND A FISH?
A PAIR OF SWIMMING TRUNKS!

WHY IS A CLASSROOM LIKE AN OLD CAR ?
BECAUSE ITS FULL OF NUTS WITH A CRANK AT
THE FRONT   FROM MICHELLE MILLS

So i went to the dentists. He said "Say aaaaah." I said "Why?" He said. "My dog's died."

Police arrested two kids yesterday. One was drinking battery acid and the other eating fireworks. They charged one and let the other one off.

-I LOST MY DOG
-WHY DON'T YOU PUT AN AD IN THE PAPER?
-DON'T BE DAFT, HE CAN'T READ

HOW DO U NO THERE'S A ELEPHANT UNDER YUR BED? COZ YUR NOSE IS TOUCHING THE CEILING! BY SCOTT JENNINGS

THIS DOG, IS DOG, A DOG, GOOD DOG, WAY DOG 2 DOG KEEP DOG A DOG THICK DOG PERSON DOG BUSY DOG 4 DOG 30 DOG SECONDS DOG. NOW SAY IT WITHOUT DOG!!

Q: how do u make a sausage roll?
A: push it down a hill! by piggs

1. What happens if u walk under a cow?
U cld get a pat on the head!
2. What's yellow and smells of bananas?
Monkey sick.
(Samantha Lister)

WHAT DO U CALL A HORSE WITH CLOTHES ON?
A CLOTHESHORSE. HA HA.

What is mary short for?
she has no legs! Ha ha ha ha!
From jo birch!

What do you get if you cross a cow, a sheep and a goat. A milkey bar kid

"Doc, I can't stop singing the 'Green, green grass of home.'" "That sounds like Tom Jones syndrome." "Is it common?" "It's not unusual."

WOT DO U CALL A RUSSIAN FIZZY DRINKS THIEF ?.   HOODYA NIKAPOPOV

WHAT DID THE DOG SAY 2 THE FLEA? answer: DONT BUG ME! leah

How many men does it take to decorate a bedroom? Between 1 and 10, it just depends how thin you slice them.......

THERE IS TWO PARROTS SITTING ON A PERCH AND ONE PARROT SAYS TO THE OTHER DOESNT THIS PERCH SMELL FISHY TO YOU. FROM MARK WHITE.

Could u teach me how to send
a text message

Two men walk into a pub... oops thats
wrong let me thing again two men oh
wait thats right so heres the joke aaaah
forgot the punchline. goodbye

Mental anxiety, Mental breakdowns,
Menstrual cramps, Menopause... Did you
ever notice how all women's problems
begin with MEN!?!?!?   (Hannah Mac x)

NASTY NIGEL...PICK ME

what has a neck BUT NO HEAD? a bottle

MY FRIEND WORKS IN A CHIP SHOP+SHE HAD
AN AWFUL TIME.   THERE WAS A FITE.
THE FISH GOT BATTERED!

Man walks into a bar... Bet that hurt.

THERE IS A REASON Y THERE IS A BANANA
IN MY EAR-IM TRYING 2 LURE
THE MONKEYOUT OF MY HEAD

What do u call an Italian man
with a rubber toe?
Roberto!!

What do you call a man with
no underpants?
Nicholas

Q: What do u call a woman who throws
her mobile phone bills on the fire?
A: BERNADETTE

How many letters in da alphabet?
22 - JR got shot & ET went home.

Wot did the little lite bulb say 2
the mummy lite bulb??
I wuv u watts+watts!

If u put this on the tv does it
make it a tellytext?

Roy Keane says to Fergie "I've got t
have a cortisone injection". Becks says
"if he's getting a new car i want
one 2 boss".

DID U HEAR ABOUT THE IRISH BURGLER WHO
WORE WHITE WELLIES SO HE WOULDN'T
LEAVE TRACKS IN THE SNOW.

WAT IS GREEN + BOUNCES?
A SPRING ONION

DER R 3 TYPES OF PEOPLE IN DIS WORLD:
THOSE WHO CAN COUNT AND
THOSE WHO CAN'T.

Japan Ban

Despite the popularity of SMS as a means to woo voters in other parts of the world, MPs in Japan are actually banned from using their mobile phones to send or receive text messages or e-mails during debates in parliament. Sessions had become so boring that some MPs were using their phones to text friends and colleagues to relieve the tedium – but if this sounds cheeky, bear in mind that other less subtle politicians had taken to reading newspapers or novels if the discussions became too dull. (Books and papers have been banned too.) Younger MPs objected to the SMS ban as they said their phones were essential for quick and up-to-the-minute communications – and for staying awake during parliamentary debates...

Wot is orange + sounds like a parrot?
A carrot!

What is rubarb? Embarrased celery

Y DID THE NURSE TIPTOE PAST
THE MEDICINE CABINET
BECAUSE SHE DIDNT WANT TO
WAKE THE SLEEPIN PILLS

Woman found dead in bath tub filled
with milk & cornflakes. The police r
looking 4 a cereal killer.

OFFICIAL SIGN ON DOOR 'DOOR ALARMED'
HAND WRITTEN SIGN NEARBY
'WINDOW FRIGHTENED'!

If the whole world is a stage where do
the audience sit

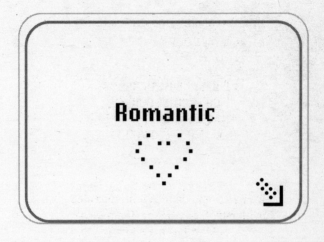

You = Gorgeous
You = Sexy
You = Intelligent
You = delicious
You = Seductive
Me = Liar
But I still luv ya!
to my darling ronnie, luv you so much
always from andrea xxxxxxxxxxxx

To Jack Ryder...
I wish i was a teddy bear which layed
upon your bed. So everytime u cuddled
it u would cuddle me instead.
Clare Thurley Aylesbury

U R 2 good 2 B 4 gotten!

xcuse me, could u tell me the directions
to your heart..(K)(K)(K)

lee, i've fancied you since i first set
eyes on you! you're absoloutley
gorgeous!!! ps i miss your curls babe!!!!
love seanne xxxx

I love noel sullivan from hearsay
i love noel sullivan from hearsay
i love noel sullivan from hearsay
i love noel sullivan from hearsay
Lu meeeee
xxx

i love lola in lampetre school

My eye$ reacted and my mind wa$
attracted, my heart wa$ affected,
thou$ands were rejected, but YOU! $exy
wa$ the one i $elected

roses r red violets b blue ur so sweet
and it would b a dream 2 go out
wiv u luv ?

: I can but speak of love to thee,
: for thou art all of love to me.
: I can but sing to stars above,
: for Darrel is my one true love.

when i 1st touched u i was scared to kiss
u. When i 1st kissed u i was scared to
love u and now that i love u i am scared
to lose u xxx

Russian for i love you is
"Katja, ja tebja lublu"
Sent by lgs

royston higdon will you marry me i'm
sorry i turned you down i was stupid u 2
me r everything joanne

Symon Chittenden-Symon honey i love
you and will do 4eva-will you marry
me?love Laura

Mr tickle, how about u jump of a cliff
with me in the summer. Just remember
the ropes! Creamy

could u please tell the world that 10 years ago i found the love of my life my partner charlie love u always john

Laura + Mark from Dover met, txt every day 4 8 months, run up joint bill of £1,400 now in love, living together and owe it all 2 'joy of txt'

my lips are feelin really lonely today can yours keep em company?

myfanwy will you marry me?

ULRIKA will u marry me???
Mick (Farnborough)

I've seen angels in the sky, i've seen snow fall in july. I have seen things u only imagine to see or do but I still aven't seen anythin as beutiful as u.

To live dis life i need a heartbeat, to have a heartbeat i need a heart, to have heart i need happiness, to have happiness i need u!

A rose 4 U
---"{@

JOHN. I WANT THE WORLD TO KNOW I LOVE YOU JEANETTE XXXXXXXXXXXXXXXXXXXXXX

If friendship could be bought or sold, as if it was stocks and shares. Those wise enough to invest in you, would all be Millionaires.

kisses blown r kisses wasted. kisses rnt kisses unless they r tasted, kisses spread germs germs r h8ed so kiss me baby im vaccinated!!!!!!!

Julie B.
My angel, my soulmate, my love…you
are my cherished, sweetheart.
All my love
Dan
xxxxxxxxxxx

my tears have gone cold, yet i stll hold
on to the feling that u'll come back to
me….deep within my soul

Gemma I luv U from the tip of yor nose
to the end of yor toes. U R my Angel,
Big H+C+XXX Lorcan

YYs UR YYs UB, ICUR YYs 4 me

X I LOVE YOU X
XXX   from   XXX
XXXXX ME XXXXX
XXXXXXX C U XXXXXXX

Don't Panic...

A teenage student in Japan was leaving college slightly later than usual, and being a responsible girl, she texted her father to let him know she was getting on the bus and on her way home. 'I'll tell you if my bus is hijacked,' she joked. Unfortunately, her father completely misread the message and rang the police, telling them that there was a hijacker on board the bus. He frantically tried to ring his daughter again and again to find out if she was all right, but there was no answer. Within half an hour the police had mobilised 46 patrol cars in a massive operation to resolve a potentially tragic situation. Fortunately, a short while later, her dad re-read the message and realised, with a mixture of relief and horror, that he'd got the wrong end of the stick. He made a very sheepish phone call to the police to let them know of his mistake, but he still couldn't understand why his daughter hadn't answered her phone. In the end it turned out that she had been too polite – she didn't want to irritate the other passengers on the bus. (We aren't told whether becoming embroiled in the centre of a police operation with 46 patrol cars and trained marksmen irritated the passengers at all.)

Alan, I am sorry for the hurt. I want you
back and miss you loads. VV = me on my
knees! Love you know who! xxxxx

COS I LUV U HONEY
--'--¨---{@
LOOK SIDE WAYS

Bright Eyes I Love you more
now than I did in Prague.
Chris

A night without you is
like a day without
sunshine...

We go together like a
wink and a smile

Night night till thee fair eyes close into
the world of dreams.

My daughter Michelle met her boyfriend
Simon via text messaging - 9 months
later they are still going out!!
Miriam Daniel

shortest word is
I sweetest word
is LOVE cutest
person is YOU

my life is alphabet.
1 thing is missing is U

God in heaven, God above protect the
person that i love, sent with a smile
sealed with a kiss, i love the person
who is reading this

many people will walk in and out of
your life but only true friends will leave
footprints in your heart.......
you left yours in mine XXXX

I can't txt u roses nor fax u my h rt, i'd
e-mail u kisses but we'd stil B apart, i
luv u2 bits jus wish u cud C, i c re 4U so
much, U mean da world 2 me...

If a kiss was a raindrop id send u
showers!If a hug was a second id send u
hours!If a smile was water id send u the
sea!If love was a person id send u me! x

ROSE I LUV U BUT I DONT WANT 2 SPLIT
U&CRIS UP LUV MAT

if i cud send just 1 text it wud b 2 my
wife caroline 2 tell her i still luv her
after 18 months apart i no she hated me
but i want her back so much
phil beaman

I wish i were ur tears, id b born in ur
eyes, live on ur cheeks and die on ur
lips, if u were my tears id never cry in
case id lose u! Xx

4GETIN U IZ HARD 2 DO, 4GETIN ME IZ UP 2 U,
4GET ME NOT, 4GET ME NEVA, 4GET DIS TX BUT
NOT DIS SENDA!

If I have the letters HRT I could add EA
and have a HEART or add U and get HURT
but I would rather get HURT than have a
HEART without U.

Listed below are the things that
I don't like about you:
1.
2.
3.
4.
5.
6.
7.
8.
9.
10.
11.
12.
13.
14.
15.
16...
Wat can I say?
I LUV evrythin bout U...honest

SMILE!..'cause you just got a message
from someone who luvs u!

Last nite i wantd 2 write t a poem but all
i cud write was. . . "noh ss!w !" didnt
make sense until i read it upside down.

Amongst all the stars in the sky the
most precious one i can say is mine!
Amongst all the dreams that must come
true my only dream is to have
someone like you!

A= ur attractive
B= ur brave
C= ur cute
D= ur a darling
E= ur exciting
F= ur fabulous
G= ur so great
,)) ,″,″,″,″,
(,") . "MWAH".
")″″″.″.″.″."

James Hobbs please would you do me
the honour of saying yes 2 marrying
me? All my love David Babbington. MCC
church will do the ceremony!

SOMEONE DROPPED A TEAR IN THE
OCEAN WHEN THEY FIND IT THAT'S
WHEN I'LL FORGET YOU

Tell little laura that i love her more
than words can describe.
From a little southerner. X

WE HAVE SOMETHING WE WOULD LIKE TO ASK
TINO FROM NEWCASTLE THERE R 3 OF US
FANCY HIM WHICH ONE DOES HE LIKE THE
BEST? SAM PAMELA OR SARAH?

My Sexy Baby! I luv u with all my "3!
Nearly 3yrs baby! Uve made me so
happy! Cant w8 2 our hols! luv u loads
baby! Ur squidgy *;-) xoxoxox
+millions more!

Chokky! Now U have the time U Just Need the place. A haven of Peace! A Palm fringed Paradise awaits. Take the next dream bus 2 find a Rainbow in the Moonlight.X

IF U & ME HAD NEVER MET THEN ALL MY LIFE I WOULD REGRET 4 ME &U WERE MEANT 2B

Hello,txting is an enjoyable way to communicate, and my now fiance even txt me his marriage proposal from outside my frount door! from Nadine in Harrow Middx.

```
      ""
(",)  This Ant is
"( )" looking 4 u
,,J L,,
  "" and SHE
(,") misses u a
/( )" lot...
,,J L,,
  //
(,")"   WHY?
"( )'
,,J L,,
coz ur so SWEET!
```

God made butter God made cheese God made U 4 me to squeeze God made whisky God made pepsi But when God made U....... DAMN! He made YOU SEXY!

Summons 2b in cupids court chrges No1:STEALIN my heart. No2:TRESPASSIN in my drms. No3:ROBBING me of my senses. If guilty sentnce 2life with me. How do u plead?

Mike from Weymouth. I found my wife was having an affair when I found the bill - she had sent him 149 in 4 weeks! I got divorced last week!

To deb. When is our baby going to show up. Tell baby they are now overdue.

I WANT A BABY JASON SHAW WHAT DO U SAY LUV JO

Yvonne Ryan I gave you everything
because I love you. I hope you find
courage too

Text is good text is fine lets hope the
BBC prints mine!! I love Amanda
Whitbread.Steve)

NOT SURE HOW U WANT THIS, BUT I MET MY
LOVER BY SENDING A TEXT MEANT 4 SOMEONE
ELSE HE IS MY MR DARCY AND IM HIS
BRIDGET, WE TEXT ALL THE TIME

Andy i just want to say thank you for
being there for me and my son
we love u Fiona

CHRIS U MADE ME WANT TO LOVE AGAIN!
I LOVE YOU ALTHOUGH I HAVENT MET YOU I
HOPE WE DO MEET LUV SAM

ANDREW I 4GIVE U! KEEP ASKNG COS I MAY
SAY YES 4 REAL ONE DAY...STEADY
SWEETHEART! CAYTE X X X

BEKY I REALY LUV U WIL U GO OUT WIV ME?
U KNOW WHO! d;)

i meet my boyfriend of a year + half
though text msg's. I got a number
wrong when sending my msg + we
flirted + talked. Then met up + the
rest is history. :-)

It takes 2 to tango, 2 to kiss,
2 to talk & reminisce, so many good
things come in 2, & one of those
things is me & u!

There are tulips in my garden,
there are tulips in the park,
but nothing is more beautiful then
our two-lips meeting in the dark!

Red Alert

SMS alerts have become very popular as companies look for new ways to give their customers a better service (i.e. make money and promote their product). Everyone knows that you can get the latest football scores sent to your mobile (for a hefty charge each time) but did you realise that you can also get text messages detailing your bank balance and warning you if you go overdrawn? Certain banks are introducing the service for a monthly fee for all those customers who really want to be depressed by the sight of their financial plight every time their phone beeps at them. And Trekkies are being encouraged to immerse themselves in the Star Trek universe by signing up to receive free cheats via SMS for a recent Star Trek computer game.

But however much of a waste of good technology this may seem, some organizations are finding the instant communication afforded by SMS can be put to good purpose. London's commuters can sign up to receive free alerts of Tube travel chaos twice a day warning them of the nightmare journey ahead of them, while Nottingham's bus users can key in a particular number code for the bus stop they are at and a text message will come back telling them how long they have left to wait for their bus. The National Blood Bank sends its volunteer blood donors messages to remind them when they are due to give blood, and Amnesty International members can receive urgent action SMS alerts, with brief details of individuals at risk of torture and their whereabouts. They can then add their names to an electronic petition or send an automatically generated e-mail to the relevant government or authority to help protest against human rights abuses throughout the world.

Firefighters in Holland have taken the possibilities of SMS one step further and are piloting a scheme which will directly affect the safety of the deaf community. The Dutch fire brigade will send SMS alerts to deaf people in Amsterdam at the same time as they sound the city's disaster siren. The message 'Go inside and close doors and windows' will be sent to all mobile phone users registered on the scheme. If the system's a success, it will become standard throughout the country.

If I ad 3wishes Id giv away2. Al I need is1
so I can wish 4u!

Candy Floss?

Nope!

Chocolate?

Nah!

Let me see...

How bout Sugar?

Hmm...
Nope!

Damn!

Still cant find nothing as SWEET as U!

I would text my husband wherever he
was to say I loved him & to get the dinner on! ;o)

 102

T only person that id send a txt msg 2 is my fiancÈe who i met via txt n were now engaged n in t process of gettin a house. txt love works

lv liked lots ov thingz, but luvd very few but no 1 haz been as special as u, id stand & wait in the worldz longest Q, just 4 the pleasure of being close 2u.XxX

U CAN FALL FROM A MOUNTIAN, U CAN FALL FROM A TREE BUT THE BEST PLACE TO FALL IS IN LUV WITH ME!

Hi 2 michael wright! Remember Whitney Houston,Saving all my love 4 u.please get in touch.miss u always.

Lee B - Thanx 4 bein there that nite. I know weve not known each other but I think ur gr8! (Is that cheesy?) Luv ya! xx xx :-

If leaves were smiles,
i'd give u a tree.
If water were kisses,
i'd give u the sea.
and if friends were 4eva,
i'd give you me.

Some1 somewhere dreams of ur smile
and while thinking of U says life is
worth while so when ur lonely
remember its true some1 somewhere
is thinking of U! xxx

Another month,
Another year,
Another smile,
Another tear,
Another winter,
A summer too.....
But there'll
Never be.......
Another friend
Like you!!!:*

Kay
4
Shiv

Friendship is like a glass,
handle it with care,
once its broken its hard 2 repair
Always remember that the torn heart
can bleed but never 4get

"Friends r angels, from above sent by
god 4 us 2 love. So when your lonely,
sad, or blue remember i'll b there 4 u"!
Danielle smart, Bishop's Stortford.

Never change for anyone, and never
expect anyone to change for you.

friends r like stars!
****
****
u cant always c them but
there always there!
Julie H, Kent

Holy mother full of grace, bless my
boyfriends gorgeous face, bless his hair
that tends to curl, keep him away from
other girls....

Mark.U R perfect!I couldnt live without U!LOVE U ALWAYS Me x

ANGEL(BUFFY) I AM YOU WINGS. LUV MEL. X X

LOVE IS AGELESS

**Thoughtful
!!!**

WHAT IS... Greater than God, More evil
than Satan, Poor people ave it, Rich
people need it, if you eat it you will die?
ANSWER: NOTHING!

R WE FRIENDS OR R WE NOT U TOLD ME ONCE
BUT I 4GOT AND IF I DIE B4 U DO ILL GO TO
HEAVAN N WAIT 4 U.

I would love to txt andrea bocelli.
I've bn afan of his4 ages + wold
relly lk 2 mt him!
From Margaret, in cirencester

He who asks a question may be a
fool 4 5 mins, he who does not may
b a fool 4ever.
JMB

It's nice to be important - but it's
more important to be nice!
-Tara from NEWPORT

Everyl's different, so it's
abnormal to be normal!
BH

i wood tex my cuz,she died wen she
was 7 and on bearly saw her.i wool love
to no if shes ok and if she has any pain
left?love ya michelle xxxxx!!
Dawn Kent

Is this what society has become reduced
to. Unable to communicate properly we
must text shortened words to each
other. what is wrong with talking?

To the world you might be one person,
but to one person you might be the
world. :)

If wisdom grew on trees, surely Tony
Blair would be a bush.

Too Chicken

SMS promotions from fast food chicken restaurants in one large shopping complex have provoked a few raised eyebrows from customers. Text messages asking 'Are you a breast or a thigh man?' were sent to mobile phone users by one restaurant, while another wanted to have someone dressed up as a giant chicken wandering around the mall, and text customers with the message 'Visit our big cock for promotional vouchers'. But this was felt by the authorities to be in egg-ceptionally bad taste and the idea was shell-ved.

We never fail. We only suceed in making
a mistake! =0)

I'll never float like a butterfly, nor sting
like a bee, but I thank you as my hero
Mr Muhhamed Ali.

Keep your friends close, but
your enemies closer still.

The two most abundant things in the
universe are Hydrogen and stupidity.

Heartbreak is the worst feelin in
the world. It is universal pain. But love
is the best feeling in the world. It is
universal happiness.

God made us plain and simple, but we
have made ourselves complicated.

Smile thay said, life could be worse, so I
did, and it was!

make new friends
but keep the old
1 is silver
the other is gold
nina

christina aguilera
i would ask wot woz she thnkin wen she
got an afro? She luks like a
poodle!!!!

Today, is the tomorow you worried
about yesterday......
faye (york)

the harder you think the more you find
theres no real answer!

The real problem with SMS messaging
that I fins is that the users are
limited to a maximum of only as many
as 160 letters per messa

A word of wisdom, "If you do not have
what you want, then you must like what
you have" Romanian Probverb

In life, only 3 things are worth a damn:
Love, Happiness and Friendship. And
they are all 1 and the same.

If i were a tear in ur eye i would roll
down ur face & stop at ur lips, but if u
were a tear in my eye i would never cry
coz ill b 2 scared 2 lose u.

xxx

a lie can travel halfway around the
world while the truth is putting its
shoes on - Mark Twain

Wil U Go Out W My Frnd?

In a mobile phone survey of over a thousand sixteen- to eighteen-year-olds, most teenagers said they expect to get at least one message every day. And it probably won't have anything to do with current affairs, the economy or politics – not a single one claimed to receive news alerts on their mobiles. Instead it seems that teenagers are using text messaging to improve their love lives: over half the boys surveyed said they use SMS to ask girls for a date. Less intimidating than asking a girl out face-to-face, and infinitely cooler than the 'will you go out with my friend' ploy, texting for a date is apparently the teenage boy's solution to shyness. Under a fifth of girls admit to asking boys out in a text message: girls use SMS to talk about boys instead. Nearly half use texting to discuss friends and love lives, compared to only three per cent of boys. A whole lot of gossip can fit in 160 characters.

the sun the moon and the stars
would have disappeared long ago had
they been within easy reach of
human hands.

William Hague: You are the weakest link
- good bye :-)

Hello everyone! Treat life how you want
it to treat you! Good Luck In Life!

Laugh @ yourself, b4 some1 else does.

Whether you think you can or you think
you can't, you're right.
Henry Ford

I try to take things one day at a time...
But lately several days have attacked
me at once!

Among life's dying embers these
are my regrets:
When I'm "right" no-one remembers,
When I'm "wrong" no-one forgets.

The 160 character limit does not
dumb down. It reflects the
restraint of the Haiku.

A PRETTY DOOD RULE IN LIFE IS THAT
WHATEVER IS THE HARDEST THING TO DO IS
PROBABLY THE RIGHT THING TO DO.

Many a true word
said in txt !

Any one can die, the hard bit is living.

Someone who thinks
logically provides a
nice contrast to the
real world.

If you always do what you have always done, you will always get what you have always got.

Life is like a giant canvas-throw all the paint you can at it!! H

To live is to suffer and to survive is to find the meaning of the suffering.

God grant me the serenity to accept the things I cannot change, Courage to change the things I can and Wisdom to know the difference

If practice makes perfect, and nobodys perfect, why practice?

"life's 2 short 4 wasting, 4 'ifs' + 'might have beens' + life's 2 short 4 wondering if u could have lived ur dreams."
luv Soph x

Studying the Text

You can now take a degree in Golf Tourism and Airline Catering (if you really want to) and it's quite possible that SMS Studies will soon be on the syllabus. Students at Nottingham University have conducted a study on SMS English, trying to discover if there are any rules or patterns in text messaging. After looking at hundreds of messages, they have concluded that there is no real pattern, which they believe could be for a number of reasons. Firstly, it's only been around for a few years. Secondly, it's apparently a 'youth thing': SMS is most popular with young mobile phone users, with seventy-seven per cent of all messages being sent by fourteen- to sixteen-year-olds. Thirdly, it's hard to establish rules of language in 160 characters. And finally, they were probably too busy looking at what the message said rather than how it was written – apparently forty per cent of all students with mobile phones use SMS to send sexy or flirty messages.

A view on War!
"Those that we fight we do not hate,
those that we guard we do not love"

Kung Fo Mink say: "Earth provides
enough to satisfy every man's need, but
not for every man's greed"

We make a living by what we get. We
make a life by what we give.
W.Churchill

"We can do no great things, Only small
things with Great Love"
Mother Theresa

i
(little angel)

I wonder - does Tony Blair text?

MY ? WOULD BE 2 BILL GATES?
HOW DID U DO IT?

I'd text Victoria Beckham 2 ask how she
got her figure back so quick after
Brooklyn. I had my baby 11 weeks ago
and am still a stone over weight. Jennet
xxx

If i could txt anyone i would txt
the inventor of txt enabled phones
to tell them they are a genius!
from rachael merluk

If could txt ne1 id txt eminem n id ask im
if i could sing a duet @ 1 of his concerts
wi im. Then id ask if we could go 2
McDonalds 4 a meal. Luv Hannah Watson

I would send a text to my sister in the
south of france who has quinceys sayin
get better soon sis! Love you sian xx

i want to say thanks to andrew
philipson from ashton high school,
he's nicest guy from kate.

I THINK OF MYSELF AS A STRAIGHTFORWARD
RESPONSIBLE HUMANBEING BUT WITH THE
SOUL OF A, CLOWN WHO ALWAYS SEEMS TO
FAIL AT THE MOST CRUCIAL OF MOMENTS

If I could meet any one in the world it
would be Tony Blair & I would tell him to
sort his life out from Duncan

Dear steven spielberg i am the actress
you need for you next big movie just
cannot find the place to start please
please check me out!

i would like 2 txt lance armstrong
(cyclist) 2 ask where how he managed 2
overcome cancer. where did he get his
strength from 2 beat it?

I would send a text message to
alexander graham bell and say why
didnt u think of this dumb bell

TO GOD...DO U XIST?

I WOULD TXT MY BEST FRIEND NATALIE MOGG
BECAUSE WE HAD A ARGUMENT.

I wud send a text to myself
because i'm cocky.

IF I COULD TXT ANYONE I WOULD TXT DAVID
BECHAM AND ASK HIM WHAT IT FEELS LIKE TO
SCORE THE WINNING GOAL IN A FOOTBALL
MATCH FROM CHRIS CURTIS

CAN SUM1 TELL TREV RANDLE FROM COV THAT
ITS A BOY YEAH !

TO D COULTHARD U WILL WIN THE GP IF RON
& ADRIAN TELL MIKA IT IS PAYBACK TIME.
GOOD LUCK U WILL B F1 WORLD
CHAMPION THIS YEAR.

I would text Ulrika and ask her what she
is doing next Saturday ;o)

I asked God 4 a
Flower
he gave me a garden
I asked 4 a tree
he gave a forest
I asked 4 a river
he gave me an Ocean
I asked 4 an ANGEL
he gave me U!

TO TONY BLAIR.. CUT THE SPIN
THIS TIME AROUND!

HELLO. MY FRIEND HELLO. JUST THOUGHT ID
LET YOU KNOW COME SING AGAIN TO
SHEFFIELD AND MAKE MY HEART GLOW
to neil diamond-from maria

```
        ><(((;>
        o
        o
        o
        0 ><(((;>
        o
        o
        o
        0 ><(((;>
        o
        0
        0
        o
        0 <;)))><
        0
```

**I swam the deepest ocean
just to tell U that I MISS U!**

**a good friend is like a good bra...
hard to find, comfortable,
supportive,prevents you from falling,
hold U tight, and always close 2 ur
heart..!! UR MY BRA :)**

**I would like 2 text prince william and
ask him 2 marry me love sarah**

Some people seem to spend more money texting than they would if they actually called the people and spoke to them! True? Mike in Grimsby.

I would wamt to text sean connery & ask him to come home to scotland and take me to his fav restaurant

I'D LIKE 2 TEXT RICKY MARTIN SO I COULD ASK HIM 2 TAKE ME SALSA DANCING.

I would most like to have a one 2 one with mr potato head

I'D SEND A MESS 2 W.HAGUE. DHSS OPEN 9.00am MON. MORN.

We would ask the queen -what toilet paper do you use? - rick & stew in Blackburn

On earth there's heaven U just
need 2 find the door

i WUD txt elvis asking where r u ?

Go placidly among the noise + haste,
+ remember what peace there may be in
silence + as far as possible without
surrender, be on good terms with
all persons.

o to think that tv has dedicated a whole
night to text messaging means that at
long last the world has finally gone
mad! Joanna Moone age 25 x

I'd txt Robbie Williams and ask him if he
thinks Port Vale will ever get into the
premiership - KIM FROM LICHFIELD

Jennifer Lopez will u marry me
-Mark Hicks

I'd text George Lucas 4 a part in
the new star wars film!

i can't hide this from u anymore i really
don't wanna hurt u but i feel its better i
tell u be4 u hear it from someone else
i'm really sorry but theres no santa

I would like to text beckham as
i have just cut my hair like him
from wayne in london

You sad cases texting on
a saturday night

I Would send a text message to Eric
Clapton because I want some guitar
lessons from GOD from David Bates

If i could txt ne1 it would b jonathon
ross.I wood ask him how he copes not
saying his rs.I cant and my friends say i
wont be famous.Amanda.15.Kent 8>)

Generation Text

And now for some more frightening statistics: nearly half of all children in the UK aged between seven and sixteen own a mobile phone. Parents buy them for the safety aspect, happy that they can get in touch with their children 'just in case', but nearly all young phone owners said they used their phones to text their friends rather than keep them for an emergency. They don't make many voice calls which are more expensive, using their phones instead to send on average three text messages a day. However, SMS alone can build bills of frightening proportions: one fifteen-year-old in Nottingham ran up a phone bill of £151 in one month just by texting her friends. At 10p per message, this works out at 1,510 messages for the month – about fifty every day. Another Liverpool teenager sends on average a thousand text messages each month, claiming that she's a SMS addict. She has taken a Saturday job to pay for phone vouchers to supply her £1,200-a-year 'habit'. Apparently she even takes the phone to the toilet with her. But now parents are biting back: over three-quarters of teenagers said they are sent messages about their behaviour. Parents are most likely to text their children messages telling them to be home at a certain time, and also text them warnings about drinking, smoking, homework and sex. Not surprising, then, that the gadget most teenagers now want on their phones is an SMS service they can turn off!

To the rolling stones. Can i be your bass
player for just 1 song during ur next tour

IF I COULD SEND A MESSAGE 2 ANYONE IN THE
WORLD IT WOULD B "JAMIE OLIVER". 2 ASK
HIM 2 COOK MY TEA 4 ME. I'M HUNGRY!. FROM
CHAR IN PLYMOUTH.

Hello! :-) i'd like 2 ask Ronan Keating
would he ever consider doing 1 big
concert 2 end Boyzone years once & all

I WOULD LIKE TO MEET MICHAEL SCHUMACHER
AND SHAKE HIS HAND AND WISH HIM ALL THE
BEST FOR THE SEASON FROM CARL H

I'd ask dale winton for the lottery
numbers ! Giffy S-Wales

PLEASE CAN U SAY HELLO TO SUE FOSTER
FROM HER LOVING DAUGHTER RACHAEL
FOSTER IN SOUTHPORT

William shakesphere on b half of all
school children y just y ?

STEVE COOGAN- SUM1 ACTUALLY WANTS A
DATE WITH ALAN PARTRIDGE SUGGEST OWL
SANCTUARY 4 GOOD NITE OUT - TXT JAYNE

Tony Blair: You've been given a 2nd
chance: make it count. Improve the
NHS-its our best attribute! Make it a
priority-don't waste your chance!
Good luck x x x

Mr Bush - Can i have a look
around the White House.
Yours Mark

Antony Worrall Thompson-U R gorgeous.
xxx
Love Nicky Dark.

WILLIAM HAGUE YOU SHOULDNT GIVE UP YOU GAVE SOME OF US HOPE FOR THE FUTURE THE REST OF YOUR PARTY LET U DOWN AND U DESERVED BETTER GOODLUCK FOR THE FUTURE X

CARTMAN FROM SOUTH PARK: YOU'RE NOT BIG BONED JUST FAT!

MY BOSS. PLEASE DONT SACK ME!

Nelson Mandela: If you could explain the experience of being freed in only one word what would it be?
From Ruth Denton

Eddie Izzard cheers for making me laugh until it hurts all these years. :-)

ALBERT EINSTEIN- PROBABLY YOUR GREATEST MISTAKE WAS BEING CLEVER.

I WUD TXT TUPAC SHAKUR AND ASK HIM WEN HES COMIN OUTA HIDIN CUZ I DONT BELIEVE HES DEAD AND I HAVE EVIDENCE! TEHE! URS DANIELLE TOPPING!

I WOULD TEXT TONY BLAIR. I WOULD ASK HIM IF HE WOULD CONSIDER GETTING THE YOUNG PEOPLE MORE INVOLVED IN THE VOTING PROGRESS. WHY? I'VE VOTED ONCE & I'M 31. ANGIE

I would txt M. schumacher and ask to borrow his ferrari 4 a day. (660FR)

I WOULD TXT KURMIT THE FROG TO ASK HIM IF MISS PIGGY IS O.K *JULIANNE EDISS FROM SOUTHAMPTON

if people sometimes get u down & u want 2 have sum fun then wear a smile 4 a little while & they will wonder wot uve done

I WOUD LUV 2 ASK WHITNEY HOUSTON THE
PHONE NO OF HER DENTIST. JOANNE WHITE
OF PONTYPOOL.

IF I COULD TXT NE1 IN THE WORLD IT WOULD B
THE KILMARNOCK FOOTIE SQUAD TO TELL
THEM THAT I LOVE THEM NO MATTER WHAT
THE RESULT FROM DEBBIE NAGLE

Wotz up people. The world of txt is just
da best. Cum on expres ur self. Or
should i say TXTPRESS UR SELF !!

IM ONLY SMALL BUT, MY DAD SAY'S
WHEN THE ICECREAM MAN RINGS HIS
BELLS, HE'S RANOUT OF ICECREAM!
IS THIS TRUE?.
ZACK. PAIGNTON, DEVON.

The good thing about txt, getting a
surprise txt from a friend or a private
thought from someone special

hi zak newton in suffolk get out of the
bath now mum x x x

The twinkle in ur eyes makes my day, ur
smile makes my week, ur laugh makes
my month, ur sweetness makes my year
& ur FRIENDSHIP has made MY Life! Xx

This is a message 4 Daniel MacPherson
(Joel in Neighbours) return my
e-mails+come 2 visit my very special
pupils at Rhondda Special School.
Luv Sarah Stacey

J.K Rowling.... how do you know if you
are a wizard with muggle parents from
Matthew Newlands,

TONY BLAIR.U TAX US 2 MUCH.WE C
NO BENEFIT 2 SOCIETY.

Albert Einstein - E = MC sqrd? TXT 2 U + 4
TXT BOOK = relative fun @ home!

To Captain E.J. Smith (of Titanic) Why did you ignor all the ice warnings?

Quentin Tarantino. Pulp Fiction is an amazing film! It should have won more awards at the oscars! what inspired you to write those brilliant stories?

MR HARRISON MY HEADMASTR! HOW ABT A WK OFF?:)

Someone somewhere dreams of your smile while thinking of u feels life is worthwhile. So when u are lonley remember its true someone somewhere is thinking of you

Friends r like jewels, precious & rare, luved & respected & treated with care, friendship is a jewel of priceless design, strong as rock & constant as time.

Hi there. I am Billie from Romford and
I'd like 2 dedicate this message in
memory of my mum & nan who I loved
dearly, please put this in your book.

F.A.O Loui Theroux...investigate me!

Motto for 2001: work like you don't
need the money, dance like nobody is
watching and love like you've
never been hurt

if u save this msg,then i'm cute.if u edit
this,i'm also cute.if u 4ward ,then u're
telling people that i'm cute.but if u
erase this,u're jealous cos I'M CUTE!

:-) IT MAY NEVER HAPPEN
MY NAMES JOELLA AND IF I COULD TEXT
ANYONE I WOULD TEXT GERI COZ I THINK SHES
GREAT BUT NEEDS 2 PUT ON SOME WEIGHT!

C u on the terraces at Southend United
next season Terry.

my dad looks like william hague but
with ginger hair love lil ging

hi ever since i got my mob 1 yr ago i
havent stopped txting
bye bye xxx

People are gonna talk about u,
especially when they envy u and the life
u live, let them, u effected their life
they didnt effet urs. JMB

if my m8 cud snd a txt 2 ANY1 it wud b
davina mccall coz she is her idol & I wud
snd un 2 brian from big bro coz he's so
cute! @->- heres a rose 2 u all

You may regret what u do but u'll regret
what u dont do so much more.
JMB

Rdng & Wrtng

They may be the bane of schoolteachers' lives, and they're actually banned in many schools, but the Department for Education and Employment has started to use the mobile phone in its battle to try to improve the poor UK literacy standards. With a third of adults in Britain having the reading skills of eleven-year-olds, the Government is trying to encourage young people to enjoy reading and writing through text messaging. Pilot schemes giving free mobile phones to teenagers with the lowest literacy skills around the country have been organised and if they are successful, the mobile phone could become a standard school tool across the UK. Of course, there's an obvious flaw to the scheme – how will they ensure that the phones aren't being used to chat on? Apparently, the DfEE have thought of that, too – they're going to check the bills to make sure only SMS messages have been sent.

We wonder if David Beckhamm haz a
goochi potty ooooooooops we mean
Baby Brooklyn Sorry!!! Cat n Kat xx

I wish i was a glow worm,
A glow worm's never glum
How can you be unhappy
When the sun shines out yorbum?

Sorry Grandad if your watchin your
budgie has died the cat ate it.
Your lovin granson Martin

HARRY. CAN I BORROW URE CD

tom baker- your ther best evr dr.who
from kez

I always correctly punctuate my
messages! Guess that is the teacher
in me. Paul Mullins.

ALEX TURN ON UR FONE

SIR RICHARD BRANSON HOW R U?
HOPE U FINE!

David Beckham: How much
did ur hair cut cost.

Thomas Aquinas. If there is a real
God how do we know we've chosen the
right 1 and we're not going to meet a
vengeful lord.

GOD-where r u n y r there so many sick
people on this planet?!

I HAVE HAD A FEW TEXT MESSAGES
BY MISTAKE

CELINE DION. Y DO YOU BELIEVE THAT THE
HOT DOGS GO ON.

R u red e 4 me

MY DAD AS I HAVE NEVER MET HIM,

ALI G. MY JULIE SAY SHE NO U?

mystic meg: "will i get the job?"

SADDAM HUSSEIN   PEACE BE WITH YOU.

STEPS) COME DANCE WITH ME.

GOD IS MY PAPA AND GRAN ALL RIGHT?

SANJA i am sorry come to bed!

TINA TURNER CAN I B YUR PRIVATE
DANCER....KP

Kubrick Yr work was fantastic

Stephen hawking. Whats the secret of
the universe?

ROSEMARY CONNOLY = *PLEASE MAKE ME THIN

N. Armstrong. Can you txt
from the moon?

Bart Simpson: Eat my Shorts!

ULRIKA JONSSON I LOVE UR TOP!
WHERE DID U GET IT FROM?

JOHN LENNON.   IMAGINE.

GOD. Y ME?

J.F.Kenedy- DUCK!

Dear santa can i have a car 4 christmas?

Robbie Williams Ure gorgeous&hav a
fantastic personality! can i b ur angel?
;) xxxxx

GEORGE CLOONEY. WILL U RESUSITATE ME?

a FRIEND is:
1% funny
2% sweet
3% caring
4% loving
90% good looking...
THAT'S WHY I'M YOUR FRIEND!!!

A Message to India

Everybody hates revising for exams: there's the stress of trying to make sense of all the coursework, the headache of finding enough time to study and still have some sort of social life, and the nightmare of worrying about whether the right questions will come up. Students over the years have tried every trick to help them remember all that information, from sleeping with textbooks under the pillow to playing tapes of coursework throughout the night while they're asleep. But one enterprising young man in India didn't trust hard work or superstition and had a much better idea: don't bother revising at all, just take a mobile phone into the exam. This might have proved the answer to all his examination stress but unfortunately a teacher's suspicions became aroused when the boy kept making frequent trips to the toilet during his biology exam. On investigation the teacher discovered that the student was actually using his phone to text a family member the exam questions. This relation was armed with a host of textbooks and would look up the answers, then text them back to the student. Sadly for the student, the college didn't see the funny side and called the police!

in the nightclub i work in, the dj puts his
number on the screen & people can text
him with song requests or shout outs-it
works really well!!...luv Siobhan x

Well i think text messaging is the
greatest thing ever invented. I use the
service every day and my social life has
been improved. From kathryn soulsby.

David Beckham- England & Man Utd r a
1 man team, u dont have 2 put up with
it, cum & join scotland & chelsea
-Danny Maclaren

TEXING IS THE BEST WAY OF COMMUNICATING
WHEN U HAUED ARGURED WITH UR LOVERS
GINA

Is the art of conversation dead.
myles from bedford.

I COULDNT LIVE WITHOUT MY MOBILE!
GETTING A TXT MSG BRIGHTENS UP MY WHOLE
DAY-I JUST SPEND TOO MUCH SENDING THEM!

TOOTH FAIRY - WHERES ME MONEY?

Jesus. How long have i left-could
i get an extension

Sarah Michelle Geller - Bite Me!!!

QUEEN LIZZY WASSSSSSUP

Darcey Bussell you are the best dancer
in the world and your are my role model
laura willeyxxx

Lord Lucan. Where r u!?

Sigmund freud y r u obsesed with sex!?!

LEE STEPS U R COOL! KEEP STEPS @ NO1!
LUV SARAH WHITE.

SPICE GIRLS-WHEN IS YOUR NEXT
SINGLE COMING OUT ?

PRINCESS DIANA-R U HAPPY NOW
AND DID U LOUE DODI

ROBBIE WHICH DJ WOULD U ROCK
WITH AND WHERE !

MATT LE BLANC HOW U DOIN

HARRY POTTER. WOT DOES IT TAKE
2 B A WIZZARD?

Chrissy (my late sister) i luv u
& miss u so much. vash.xx

TONY BLAIR-IM A POOR STUDENT SORT OUT
THE FEES AND GRANTS I VOTED 4 U YA NO;-(

GODOT TIRED OF W8TING CU IN THE PUB

MR BLAIR PLEASE SAVE THE NHS

Agnetha Faltskog. we love you + your
music.Mark(ABBA FAN)!

LEONARDO DA VINCE. WAS MONA LISA
REALLY SMILING?

MICHAEL J. FOX I LUUUV AND ADORE U! LUV
TERESA.xxx. P.S.BIG KISS+HUG 2U!x.

william shakespear: to see what poetic words he could get into 160 characters.

Nelson mandela wot was it like to spend so long in prison for doing nothing wrong

CAZ-ILOVEUMUM

Mandela.U r the man!

william haque: never mind hey.

Mohammed Alfiad! Can i get a job at harrods pls :)

Terry Pratchett I'd ask him he was speciesist because only humans are undead in his books.

Big Brother is Watching You . . .

Quick to sell and easy to nick, mobile phones are one of the most popular items among thieves, and a huge number are stolen each year. But now some new software has been developed to help clamp down on phone theft. The software builds up a picture of the way you use your phone and works out the unique 'fingerprint' of each phone owner, made up of the sorts of call they make, the standard length of call, the numbers most frequently used and the time of day most calls are made. If this pattern changes suddenly, the software concludes that the phone may have been stolen and can cut it off. But just in case you're making more calls than usual because you're phoning round your friends arranging a party, don't worry: when it gets suspicious, the software sends the handset a text message, warning that it will be cut off unless your personal identification number (or PIN) is typed in immediately. And it knows enough about our phone habits to realise that New Year's Eve is a busy night for phoning and it won't cut you off then. It could be bad news for thieves – and for all those people who get drunk, make lots of phone calls to friends they haven't spoken to for years and then forget their PIN.

Bob Hoskins "It's good 2 txt ...."
@ about 2 in the morning ....

george michael.....when will u be back
in the uk touring???...michelle

VANESSA PHELPS. U LOOKIN
GOOD GIRL.(AAOHb)

BILL GATES-CAN I HAVE A LITTLE OF
YOUR MONEY PLEASE?

The inventor of txt to thank
him for inventing it

I WANT 2 TEX MEL GIBSON &
ASK HIM 2 ADOPT ME!

TO DAVID BOWIE WE ARE GETTING A PUPPY &
ARE NAMING IT AFTER ZIGGY STARDUST
I LUV U XXXXPS KEEP SINGING XX

MAGGIE THATCHER. WHEN U COMING BACK

Tny Blair.I'm hearing I hav my language+
culture.many of my friends r Deaf they r
denied both!Pls recognise British Sign
Language!Ask Deaf bout their suffering!

WHAT BENIFITS A MAN IF HE GAINS A
WHOLE WORLD BUT LOSES HIS SOUL.
ROB LEATHERBARROW

My best friend sam he died
last year i miss him

Roger. cliff richards pr. i have
been given the all clear & no longer
have cancer. thank u 4 ur support.
:) rachael ward.

Neil Armstrong- Did u really go on the
Moon or was it faked?

Paul mccartney - thnx 4 the music x

Brian conely. Its a puppet! >:3)ó

Madonna. Your so cool. Keep it real and
take it ez. Peace-xx xx xx xx

MARTIN LUTHER KING
- THANX 4 EVERYTHIN. URE MY HERO.
CUDNT HAV DUN IT WITHOUT YA

Amy - Will you forgive me? I miss
your friendship. I'm sorry I
messed everything up

Bill Gates ever wished that you had
invented the mobile phone ??

JOHN LENNON: THANK YOU.

i would txt my great uncle tony who died 2/3 weeks ago 2 say dat i love + miss him. i will alwaz love him 4ever

Dad can i raid your wallet 4 the net

TONY BLAIR: CAN I B PRIMINSTER 4 A DAY? PLZ?

Michael jackson... Can i come for tea,

ADAM ANT   YOU ARE MISSED!

Arafat/Sharo ......Why ths war?......
Try PEACE.....It ain't so BAD!!

hear'say i just want 2 say dat u r al gr8 & i cant wait 2 c u in concert wiv my 2m8s give me bc stages pases pls i luv u al so much gr8 album luv ya chrissiexx

Ann Horrocks
thanks mom i love you lots

Nelson Mandela: U R A shining star in a
world of confusion

TOM JONES WILL U GIVE ME SINGING LESSONS
FAE SALI MASSEY

THE QUEEN BCSE I WNT TO ASK HR IF SHE S
INTRSTD ABT POLOTICS

Question, if u wer stuck in Bali, what
would u rather have, ur ability 2 recieve
or send txt? Chewy

Travis - if it always rains on you,
use an umbrella

If a shop is open 24 hrs a day
365 days a year, why does it have
locks on the door?
Lee Watson

If you aim to fail, and succeed,
what have you really done?
Hayles, Chester

ITS SO GOOD THAT SOMEONE WILL SHOW THE
EFFECT THAT TXT HAS HAD. 4GET
INTERNET. THIS IS THE BIGGEST THING SINCE
MORSE CODE U DONT NEED TO FACE
ANYONE. U CAN B ANON.

How comes everyone has time to
text the programme but didnt have
time to vote on Thursday?

Im disabled and text has improve my
comuncation and I can chat up women
now. as I cant speak from Karl Dean

IVE UPSET SO MANY FRIENDS. YOU CANT HANG UP B4 U SPEAK. U HIT THE SEND BUTTON AND THATS IT. I DONT THINK WHEN I SEND. AND I SEND WHAT I THINK AT THAT SECOND. DAVE

UR F8 MAY B RITTEN, BUT UR DESTINY IZ IN UR OWN HANDZ. Mikey

Did you ever notice how many bizarre words there is in the English language, that seem to mean nothing when you use predictive text? Hmm....

I have met loads of friends by random txting u get to meet people from all over the place that ud never have met other wise! TAZx

Hello Freddy, we need you back to front Queen again. Richard from Derby.

Text Bomb

Phone theft has become a real problem in Amsterdam, with approximately three-quarters of all street robberies involving mobile phones. But now muggers are coming up against the latest anti-theft device from the Dutch police: text bombs. Once the phone is reported stolen, a specially designed police computer will bombard it with SMS warnings: every three minutes, it sends out a message to the phone saying, 'This handset was nicked. Buying or selling is a crime. Signed: the police.' Criminals have tried to get round the text bombs by removing the original SIM (subscriber identity module) card, but the system works by tracing the handset's international mobile equipment identity (IMEI) number and as soon as they get hold of this the police can start their bombing campaign, no matter how many times the thieves change SIM cards. The text bombs only stop once the phone is handed in to the police, with the idea being that criminals will be so irritated by the barrage of mail that they'll be only too pleased to give the phones back!

dont love
a friend
like a
flower,
---;-> @

bcoz a
flower
dies in
season.
love them
like a river
- - - - - - -
- - - - - -
- - - - -
- - - - - -
bcoz a river flows 4ever xxx

Did you know that 'lips' and 'kiss' are
written with the same keys?

J.K.Rowling, ACROMANTULA WARNING: get
nxt book out or we set Lethifold on u.
This is not a muggle announcement.

Warning: SMS can seriously
damage your relationship!

School teaches you a lesson in life and
life teaches you a lesson.
Dan........

i would love 2 txt Bruce Willis 2 ? him if
there's gonna b a di hard 4

To mr van dam how big r your buy-seps

Keep saying to yourself 'I'm the
best person I know'
Rick from Derby

SUCCESS: Its not the position u stand, but
the direction in which u look :-)
emaR

If kisses were water i would sent u the
sea to Andy Halsall in stafford.
Luv MelXXXX:o)

the happiest of people don't have the
best of everyfin, they just make the
most of what comes their way! :-)

GERI HALLIWELL: DO YOU WANNA BE A
CELEBRITY COUPLE GERI! COZ IM FREE
WHENEVER. I LOVE UR BIGGEST FAN
JONATHAN PENNINGTON FROM BOLTON

LEE LATCHFORD EVANS FROM STEPS
I FANCY HIM R U AVAILABLE

TO 7 OF 9 (STAR TREK VOYAGER)
WHATS IT LIKE BEING A BORG AND WHATS
IT LIKE BEING THE CORE REASON 4
WATCHING VOYAGER

THEO FOLEY. Ex Cobblers player. How R U
m8? Hope all is well? Still want UR shirt!
UR no 1 fan. Nicky Sarti

If your inner self is as beautiful as
your outer shell then you surely must
be a rose amongst the weeds a hidden
treasure from the highest spheres
of heaven...

Hi gianni ca va its Sams english friend
Nat remember! its been a long time
want 2 rendez vous will b in paris soon.
hope alls good with the gym and work
N:) x

Hi big hello 2 my m8 dani-
congradulations 2 her 4 winning
ur trophy at ur dancin show 2nite
luv ya loads stacey xxx

I thnk tht ths is a top idR n i hope u
includ ths msg luv zoe

To rolf harris:
need help my mouse <:3_)--- has
stopped working

don't you really really hate it when you
run out of characters and d
don't know where to get more from?

i love eddie izzard
he is so sexy!
bec.i. lndn

Philosophical: If a text was not
comprised of text, it would
be nameless.

Eleanor, dear daughter, Never give up
on a dream just because of the length
of time it will take to accomplish it, the
time will pass anyway. Dad xx

TAKE HEART THE ONLY PERSON WHO
ALWAYS GOT HIS WORK DONE BY FRIDAY
WAS ROBI CRUSOE

everytime you see a butterfly around,
its just me, checking if your ALRIGHT!

I would text Blackpool FC manager Steve
McMarn 2 thank him 4 a brill year

I would send a txt 2 Bob Marley
cos he's a god

If I could send any1 a message it would
b Prince Naz I would ask him what it was
like 2 win his first title

U COULD BE A SEXY SAUCEPOT WITH LOADS &
LOADS OF STYLE BUT WHAT MAKES A PERSON
SCRUMMY IS A SUPER SMASHING SMILE!

I've spent 40 quid on txts this month so
far. oops! hayleigh frm DERBY

IS THIS A RECORD? I AM 75 AND MY
SISTER IN LAW IS ALMOST 80 AND WE
TEXT EACH OTHER OFTEN.

How can u tel da rain not 2 fal wen clouds exist, How can u tel da leaves not 2 fal wen wind exist, How can u tel me not 2 fal in luv wen u exist? xxx

Brad pitt -how did ya get so fit?

Ronan Keating - Can i join u on your rollercoaster? Love M ;-)

I WOULD ASK ALL THE COUNTRIES 4 WORLD PEACE! RHYS WISEMAN ESSEX 14

SMILE!
..'cause it makes 'em wonder what the hell you've been doing!

Would ask william hague if his wife can speak

Starsky, Hutch and SMS

After a very nasty incident which left a teenager in hospital, police launched a search for his violent attacker but to no avail. Once he came off his life-support machine and started to recover, the victim was able to tell the police the identity of his assailant as they'd actually been at school together; but despite knowing where he lived and who his friends were, officers still couldn't find the thug. One thing they were able to discover, though, was his mobile phone number. Although he wasn't answering voice calls, detectives decided to bombard him with 'you can't outrun the long arm of the law'-style text messages. Astonishingly, the persistent hounding paid off: the young man gave himself up and was charged with attempted murder.

Sumtimz I think urCRAZY&totaly round DA
bend; BUTdatsOKbyME

To my grandad, if only you knew how
much it hurt not seeing u & making
peace with u b4 u died. please make
men understand life is 2 short
4 argume nts.Love U.

Thought 4 2day keep smiling ...

I hate it wen u txt sum1 & they ring u
bak 2 reply. If I wanted 2 talk 2 them I
wood hav rung em in da 1st place!

When things go wrong & when sadness
fills ur heart & when tears flow in ur
eyes, just let me know coz I want 2b
there 4 u I'm selling TISSUES BUY 1
GET 1 FREE!

I LOVE TEXTING. I TEXT AT WORK, AT HOME,
EVERYWHERE. I GET LADS NUMBERS OF
FRIENDS AND FLIRT WITH THEM. I CAN BE
ANYONE WHEN IM TEXTING, NO ONE KNOWS.
KELLY X

NELSON MANDELA...HOW DID U DO IT?

DAVID BOWIE. ANY CHANCE O A PINT

cliff richard. I luv u.

To Tony Blair. Are you having
a political party?
From Helen W (lancs)

Booby Trap

Forget Agent Provocateur or Ann Summers: the latest fashion in underwear for the third millennium is a nice sensible 'techno-bra' which can – very comfortingly – let friends or family know where to pick up the pieces if you're mugged. It's a high-tech bra made from special material that conducts electricity and can pick up any voltage change in your heart. Electronic devices concealed in gel pads then trigger a bleep noise if your heart rate rises suddenly. If you don't turn the bleep off, the system kicks into action and the bra's global positioning system (GPS) works out where you are and sends a text message to a chosen friend or member of the family detailing your where-abouts. They can either forget to open their text messages or, hopefully, phone the police to let them know your bra's gone off.

Hello I tried to fit my head in a coke can
once. It hurt!!!!! (jon W)

I asked my friend to borrow her hair clip
and she told me no

Why, why, why, why.
Does it always rain on me

Can I buy the theme tune from The Joy
Of Text? I can't get it out of my head

You can communicate when your
parents don't know your doing it! ;)

I'm sorry, I just use my machine for
phone calls. What else is there?

nobody is perfect.....i am
nobody......therefore i am perfect!

never write n e thing about a friend
b coz they always go through your
messages !!!!!!!!!!!!!

Never trust men who are short or who
have ginger hair

I enjoy standing on by beard
and making my chin sore!!!
from John Walton (beard)

adam bedingham is my name and
i like cheese but if i liked peas then
i'd be a rabbit

I'VE SENT 3 MESSAGES AND THEY HAVEN'T
SHOWN ANY OF THEM YET.

Thank you for wasting even more of
the public's time with an inane
promotion of illiteracy through
such a hateful medium.

A tiger does not take insults from sheep
- Chinese Proverb

I suppose now would be a good time
to be supportive and caring - but i
cant be arsed!

I'd love a cup of tea, if you can manage
it... God bless you! (Hilda ñ 83.
N.Stowbridge)

Quantum Mechanics:-
The Dreams Stuff is
Made of !

A little pearl of wisdom from the mind
of Chrissie Birch:
"If your parents dont have kids, then
you won't either". I need say no
more.....

hiya.
i am mickey mouse!!!
8:-)
hehehehehe!! also i am hitler!! :=)

:-) :-) :-) :-) :-)
:-) :-) :-) :-) :-)
:-) :-) ;-) :-) :-)
:-) :-) :-) :-) :-)
…there's always   one…….

al dis txt msgin lingo iz goin 2 d.t.rea8
da english langwij 1 day. so as teknolgy
getz beta we get wrse. :0) *n4in4*

If someone tells you that they always
tell lies, how do you know whether to
believe them!

Smell my Cheese !
___
oooo/
oo/
/

Wouldn't it be fun to SPEAK your text
message into your phone, rather than
all that finger stuff!

the world's gone mad!
this latest fad -
see what its progress presages:
a landscape-full
of mobile masts
so kids can swap
txt msgs

My mobile is old and as big as a brick. I
am embarrassed to take it out with me.
Is this how superficial I have become?

"Reality and normality are purely the
perception of ones own mind, in a world
that is an ever decreasing circle!"

Shall we go down the pub and have
a few drinks now means: let's go to
the pub so I can watch you
exchange 'txt msgs'!

The world is divided into
two groups of people.
Those who think the world
is divided into two groups of
people and those who don't.

Dont get 2 excited its only a txt

no credit left how sad :-(

JOHN LEAVE SALLY ALONE

I FLY TO TENERIFE ON TUES, FIRST TIME
FLYING, ANY TIPS ANYBODY FOR A NERVY
FIRST-TIMER, MAYBE I SHOULD TRY
VIRGIN AIRLINES!

Bernard phoned, he REALLY needs those
trousers back cos he's got a photo shoot
on Monday and frankly you've had them
long enough.

IF I COULD TXT ANY ONE IT WOULD BE
WILLIAM HAGE & I WOULD TELL HIM TO HAVE
AN OPPERATION ON HIS EARS FROM FISH

HELLO ULRIKA WE FROM MARS THINK UR
GREAT WEN WE TRAVEL 2 EARTH WE'LL COME
C U ALL R MARS LUV SPLARG AND UGARX

Why is it every time i call you, i always
get your voicemail

Dont cry benadictis to strangers they
might take it to heart if you really want
to get their attention sip candle wax
through a bevvy of pregnated carp

O MISSED CALLS= O MATES

Give me the power 2 text the queen
please…Im waiting

Job Text

It's difficult to look for a new job while you're at work – you don't want colleagues looking over your shoulder as you scan the papers and the internet, you can't make that important phone call in case your boss is in earshot and even e-mails aren't as private as they should be. So one recruitment consultancy has come up with the ideal solution: to text potential employees if a suitable vacancy arises. They claim it's the most discreet way possible to go job-hunting.

But if that seems like a sensible use of SMS, a woman in Derby received a text message one Sunday evening from her manager saying, 'We don't need you in work tomorrow, I'll phone you AM to explain.' She didn't hear anything so she went to her manager's office the next day, only to be told that she'd been sacked. Discreet? Or just a massive cop-out?

PLEASE SAY DAVID IS A SHUNKY
FROM HENRY NICOL

Text - the joy of... What i need is
a textaholic anonymous session

A GOOD JOKE....THE TORY PARTY?

OF ALL THE THINGS IVE LOST IN THIS WORLD
MY MIND IS THE 1 I MISS THE MOST

HEY THIS IS RACH HERE LOVIN PETE, I HAVE A
QUESTION. Y DOES DONALD DUCK NEVA WEAR
TROUSERZ YET AFTA A SHOWER HE HAS A
TOWEL ROUND HIS WAIST? WEIRD!

1 by 1 the penguins told me how they
would take over the world

Archimedes: Why bother doing all
of those equations because now
we have to do maths.

MY FRIEND JON HAS A WILY WARMER ON

SHANE FILAN FROM WESTLIFE. IF MUTANT
MONKEYS WERE FORCE FEEDIN ME DOG FOOD
WUD U SAVE ME?

:-D* I AM LAUGHING SO HARD THAT I DID
NOT NOTICE THAT A 6 LEGGED SPIDER IS
HANGING FROM MY LIP

I DID THIS
I DID THIS TO
I DID THIS TO TAKE
I DID THIS TO TAKE UP

I DID THIS TO TAKE UP SPACE

ANTONY WANTS PIES

I can't hide this from u anymore i really
don't want 2 hurt u but i feel its better i
tell u b4 u hear from somelelse i'm
really sorry but......theres no santa

IS THIS YOUR IDEA OR THE PHONE
COMPANY'S? IT'S JUST A MONEY GRABBING
SCHEME - I WON'T BE PART OF IT.

Leave me alone!

I WOULD ASK GOD IF HE CAN'T MAKE ME THIN
COULD HE PLEASE MAKE MY MATES FAT

Can u hear it?
That's your brain frying.

To the jockey of horse I backed in the
derby-'Have u finished yet ?'
Kevin Johnson

FRAN MAKES SUPERB STEAK PIE

**PREDICTION ENGLAND 2 WIN THE
WORLD CUP 2002.**

This is my thought:- these msges I keep
getting from one 2 one r annoyin! stop
txting me! also, there is no joy in txtin!
GO AWAY!!!

(To my skydiving teacher in the
Australian National Team)
- "I've tampered with your parachute".

Hi keep a bucket of cold water handy
lv caerwyn

wanna go for a walk in the woods
theresa green

Dont Eat Yellow Snow

Why was Ed wearing an ugly t-shirt
coz hes lovely?

2YYUR2YYUBICUR2YY4ME! 2WISE UR 2WISE
UB ICU R 2WISE 4ME!

England looks awful small
from over here...
Richard   Gulf of Mexico

i have discovered the joy of text

Texting is a great way to warm up
for a thumb championship

Can you bring the
Mongoose back
round again? Also,
hows the beard
since the accident?
See you at the
Mosque.

i left the country to have a bit of a break
and i come back and find out that Rory
Bremner has won the election in my
absence - tony blair

MR HAGUE IF YOUR SHORT OF SEATS WHY NOT
VISIT THE COURTS SUMMER SALE. J.J

the harder you think the more you find
there's no real answer!

Think of this, what if you spell
something wrong and the message
is Misunderstood?

SHUT UP WHEN YOU'RE TALKING TO ME!!!!

There is a fine line between fishing and just standing on the shore like an idiot.
- Scott, Sheffield

Booze is the answer.
I don't remember the question.
- Scott, Sheffield

I AM A TXT MANIAC! I TXT NOT TALK!

& now a bullfinch...tweet tweet!
From Mark

DEAR BOY HAVE YOU ANY YELLOW BALLOONS AS MY SQUIRREL HAS LOST HIS AND WITHOUT IT CANNOT GROW BANANAS

S ELLIDGE SAYS GO HOME GRANDKIDS

SMS SOS

A Scottish teenager was on the trip of a lifetime in Indonesia, enjoying the sun, sea and sand. She and the friends she was travelling with decided to charter a boat from Bali to go island-hopping for two weeks, looking for the best beaches for surfing. They set out on their trip with an experienced local crew who knew the currents, but when they reached the Lombok Strait, well known for its dreadful seas, the weather turned and the engine flooded. The storm grew apace and water started leaking in through the bottom of the boat, which was being tossed high and low on the waves and at one point nearly turned over. Fortunately, the girl remembered that she had her mobile phone with her and sent a text message home to her boyfriend in London, saying, 'Call the coastguard, we need help – SOS.' Her boyfriend called the Thames coastguard, who notified Falmouth coastguard. They in turn called the Australian coastguard, who alerted the Indonesian authorities at the embassy in Canberra. A rescue mission was set up and an Indonesian Navy gunboat was despatched to find the ship-wrecked party, finally picking them all up some time later – by which time they'd luckily managed to make it back to dry land.